The Destructive Doctrines of Our Age

Gerard M. Verschuuren

En Route Books & Media, LLC

St. Louis, MO

En Route Books and Media, LLC
5705 Rhodes Avenue
St. Louis, MO 63109

Cover credit: TJ Burdick

LCCN: 2019944153

ISBN-13: 978-1-950108-18-3
ISBN-10: 1-950108-18-X

Table of Contents

Preface

There are many doctrines around that try to change and mold our minds—doctrines such as relativism and secularism, to name just a few. They are rather dictatorial and don't allow for any other views than their own. Doctrines portray to be very reliable and solid, but in fact they turn out to be floating and fleeting opinions that have no foot to stand on. They are shaky ideologies disguised as solid doctrines. It's their disguise that lures you in.

Yet, these doctrines are very powerful—but their power is somewhat "anonymous." We may not always quite know who started them. We may not be able to point at the person who is responsible for them. We may not always even know what exactly it is that they stand for. We may not know where they came from. Sometimes they are only short-lived, but at all times they are fleeting—they just pop up, they come and go, although they leave some damage behind when they go. Even when they are short-lived, they can be quite destructive—and we may not even be aware of it.

In the meantime, we are easily sucked into their vortex. We are tossed around by their waves, making us look like rudderless, helpless, and confused people. It's actually dangerous to be exposed to them. The Apostle Paul warned us already of people being "tossed here and there, carried about by every wind of doctrine" (Eph. 4:14). People like these were not unique for Paul's era. They are still around, and will probably always be around. Not too long ago, Joseph Ratzinger, the later Pope Benedict XVI, said something similar about our own era: "How many winds of doctrine have we known in recent decades, how many ideological currents, how many ways of thinking? The small boat of the thoughts of many Christians has often been tossed about by these waves."

Fr. James Schall, S.J. once gave a sharp analysis of such ideologies. If no connection exists between what is out there and our minds, then all we know or can know is our own thoughts. And since our minds have no connection with things, we can formulate whatever world that we would like to have. From then on, we live in our own separate worlds. Our minds have no reality check, for ideologies are ideas imposed on or taken to be reality whereby what is seen and done takes place exclusively within the mind. Indeed, the world that most people now live in is an ideological world. It is a world whose limits and configuration are assembled from their desires of what they would like to be, not to what is. We are, as a consequence, forced to lie to ourselves about reality. We have to insist that abortion is not the killing of an actual human life even though every bit of evidence shows that it is. We have to insist that two members of the same sex can "marry," which is the one thing they cannot possibly do. The logical consequence of replacing reality with ideology is that no one has grounds left to correct us in what we do or say. That's why such doctrines are devastating—devastating to us individually and to society at large.

Some have compared what our society goes through with what happened at the end of the fifth century, when the once-great Roman Empire had collapsed into chaos. Barbarians invaded from the north and east, which cul-minated in the Visigoth sack of the once glorious city of

Rome in 410. Rome had seen corruption and had suffered setbacks and sieges long before the sack. But the sack itself was the decisive end of Roman order. Of course, today's West is not the Rome of 410. "This time," as Alasdair MacIntyre wrote in his 1981 *After Virtue*, "the barbarians are not waiting beyond the frontiers; they have already been governing us for quite some time." The "barbarians" of today are the disciples of modern-day devastating doctrines. They guide us along the path of accommodating and accepting the current cultural trends.

What we are dealing with here are basically ideologies. Although we don't know who started them, we do know that most of them can be traced back to the period of the Enlightenment—although some of them have a much longer history. Somehow, they have affected each one of us nowadays, Catholic or not. We have been bombarded with them in school and through the mass media—they have virtually become endemic.

It is to be expected that Christians were not immune to them and have been affected by these fleeting ideologies and destructive doctrines. Who or what can give Christians the anchor again they need to remain secured in the raging waters of the doctrines of our time? How can they arm themselves against the dictatorship of current and new ideologies? The answer is: the Catholic Church. As G.K. Chesterton put it, "The Catholic Church is the one thing that saves a man from the degrading slavery of being a child of his age."

This book will make you aware of some fifteen different doctrines that threaten us nowadays and try to keep us off track in the waters of life. We will explain how they achieve this and why they can be so destructive. Hopefully, this book can give you a reliable anchor again.

1. Relativism

What is Relativism?

You can only identify relativism if you know what it stands for. I don't want to come up with a dull, clear-cut, and seemingly precise definition of relativism here, but instead prefer to explain it in more expressive terms. Let me try it this way.

People who swear by relativism—let's call them dedicated "relativists"—claim that there is no absolute truth—there are only opinions about what is true, depending on one's point of view. Relativism denies, or perhaps just doesn't want to acknowledge, that there is something like absolute, objective truth—truth that cannot be denied or declined by anyone. The idea of relativism is promoted, for instance, by the late philosopher Richard M. Rorty: "Truth is what your contemporaries let you get away with." In other words, relativism promotes a sort of democratic ideal in matters of truth and knowledge. But this demo-cratic ideal easily turns auto-cratic. Benito Mussolini, of all people, once said, "From the fact that all ideologies are of equal value, that all ideologies are mere fictions, the modern relativist infers that everybody has the right to create for himself his own ideology, and to attempt to enforce it with all the energy of which he is capable."

Relativism is certainly not a recent invention. The ancient Greek historian Herodotus said in his book *The Histories*, "Everyone without exception believes his own native customs, and the religion he was brought up in, to be the best." Then there is another ancient Greek, Protagoras, who is known for the expression "Man is the measure of all things"—which must necessarily include any truths a person may claim. Pontius Pilate would follow soon with his legendary question, "What is truth?" Although the idea of relativism may have a long history, it was never really popular or widespread, but nowadays it is receiving more and more traction.

One of the reasons why relativism has become so popular these days is due to the impact of recent developments in biology. Because the human mind is presumably nothing more than a series of brain processes in a neuronal network—a random product of evolution, they say (see Chapter 14)—we have no way of really knowing what we think we know. There is no way anymore to distinguish fact from fiction, realities from illusions, opinions from truths, and beliefs from make-beliefs. All we claim to know as true is based on a certain pattern of neurons firing, tested in the furnace of natural selection. So we end up with mere illusions: social illusions, political illusions, moral illusions, religious illusions. In short, relativists proclaim that, in matters of truth, there is no other authority than themselves and the evolutionary past people went through. The most relativists can still accept is freedom of speech, so anyone can say whatever they want to say, true or not.

Relativism has even managed to infiltrate the strongest fortress of objective truth, science. Some philosophers of science—who are usually not scientists themselves but historians or sociologists who merely reflect on what they happen to know about science—have come up with the idea that science is not ruled by objectivity but by subjectivism, depending on the way scientists look at things. A known exponent of this view is Thomas Kuhn, who claimed that scientific ideas must be put in their sociological and psychological context to let their meaning be revealed. This is in fact another way of denying absolute, objective truth, which has been the touchstone of scientific knowledge for ages.

Kuhn made "consensus" in science a matter of mutual personal agreements codified in a so-called paradigm, shared by most members of the scientific community. Consequently, paradigm choices and paradigm changes are seen as merely depending on the subjective assent of the scientific community. Consequently, changes in paradigm may be so revolutionary that theories from different paradigms can be "incommensurable and irreconcilable," as he called it, lacking a common, objective standard to decide between them. What we have here is relativism in optima forma!

Not only has relativism infiltrated the domain of science, but also, or even more so, the domain of religion (see Chapter 2). The modern conception is that religion is a highly private issue. Since relativists tend to believe in whatever their conscience tells them to believe, truth has once more become a private, relative issue—a belief based on the philosophical doctrine that all truth is relative to the individual, especially religious truths. Relativism faithfully repeats the absolute doctrine that there are no absolute truths. The only "truth" left is what my "personal conscience" tells me it is, so *my* truth becomes *the* truth (see Chapter 6).

The end result of all of this is that relativists think of the human mind as something that *imposes* meaning on the world. In their view, there *is* no meaning in the world, no order, no causality, no rationality, no facts, no truths. All of these are merely imposed by our minds. What we see around us takes place exclusively within the mind, so our minds have no reality check. From then on, we live in our own private, separate worlds. This also holds for truth itself; it is imposed by our minds; we create truth like artists create art. Consequently, in relativism, there is no touchstone outside of us to corroborate anything we claim to be the truth.

What is wrong with Relativism?

There are many reasons why relativism cannot be true. First of all, relativism replaces truth claims with opinions and feelings. Truth is no longer a matter of facts but of opinions, convictions, and feelings. What's wrong with that? Well, if the world is round, someone's opposing opinion will not make it flat. Opinions don't trump truths. Truth is truth, even if you do not accept it; and untruth is untruth, even if you claim it. Truth is not something we create or invent, but something that we try to "capture" in the real world. Truth is the conformity of mind and reality—a match between thoughts and reality. Therefore, truth is truth—for everyone, anywhere, at any time. If relativism were true, then we would be unable to know if our daily knowledge is true or false, or what is even more striking, if our scientific knowledge is true or false. There could no longer be any dispute about what we claim to know, for we would in fact not know anything.

So what, then, is wrong with opinions? Having an opinion is like saying "I know it, but of course, I just might be mistaken," without realizing that admitting you might be wrong is admitting that you do not really know at all. If you really know something, you can no longer be wrong anymore. But in a world of mere opinions, you don't really know anything. That's the difference between truths and opinions. Again, if the world is round, then someone's opinion won't make it flat. Relativism creates moving targets and tells us to follow anything that moves. As Professor David Carlin puts it, "If there is no objective truth, we are free to believe whatever we like, including utter nonsense. And if there is no objective truth, those who have power in society are free to impose, either by persuasion or force or fraud, their beliefs and values on everybody else."

But what remains standing is that relativists basically claim that there are no absolute truths. Taken to its extreme: gravity may be true for you but not for me. As the Boston College philosopher Peter Kreeft put it, "To be a relativist, you must believe that nearly all human beings in history have ordered their lives by an illusion." He also astutely remarks about history: "There has never been a society of relativists." How can relativists promote relativism by teaching us that relativism is right and absolutism is wrong? Relativism claims everyone is right, absolutism claims some of us may be wrong. So either there is a real right and a real wrong or there is nothing wrong with being an absolutist, and nothing right with being a relativist. Kreeft then comes to a powerful conclusion, "Relativism is not rational, it is rationalization. It is not the conclusion of a rational argument. It is the rationalization of a prior action."

Second, relativism ignores the fact that our opinions cannot change facts; they cannot change the way the world actually is. Let's take science as an exemplary case. When we say that the earth is not flat, we make a statement that is either true or false. Saying the opposite, that the earth is flat, does not make the earth flat. Truth is not something we create on our own but something that we "capture" the way it *is*. Truth is not an invention but a discovery, not fiction but non-fiction. Besides, once we give up the way things are, we actually give up any form of discussion or debate. We would be entitled to claim whatever we want, for there is no final benchmark or yardstick that everyone has access to. There would no longer be any facts. And yet, almost everyone swears by the facts. Policy makers want facts, police reports are based on facts, courts require facts, science is in search of facts. All of this would crumble if there were no facts and no truths.

The Constitution gives us freedom of speech. We have the liberty to say, for example, that nicotine cannot cause cancer, but such a claim doesn't make it happen that way. Wishes and opinions don't make something true; they can't change the facts. Truth is not determined by majority votes. If truth were at the mercy of some individuals, even science would have to abandon all its truth claims. Contrary to what relativists believe, we are dealing in science with truths and facts, not sentiments, habits, or mere convictions. To cross a river, we need a bridge built by engineers with the right knowledge, not with certain habits, beliefs, opinions, or convictions; and to get into Heaven, we need faith based on the right knowledge, not on mere sentiments. G. K. Chesterton once firmly asserted "that truth exists whether we like it or not, and that it is for us to accommodate ourselves to it."

Third, here is another serious problem for relativism: it contradicts itself. We can only avoid contradiction by putting a restriction on the original claim: all truths are relative except the one of relativism. But if we do so, we should ask ourselves what entitles us to make this exception. Apparently, this position leaves us with at least one objective truth—the objective truth of relativism itself. Why not more then? The problem with a claim like "There is no such a thing as objective truth" is that it claims to be objectively true. We cannot make such a sweeping assertion without also asserting, implicitly, that there is such a thing as objective truth after all.

Denying that there is objective truth means you are

insisting in your denial that what you say is objectively true—which cannot be true by its own verdict. To say that "all truth is relative" amounts to saying that we have no way of knowing what is true. But then we have no way either of knowing that the claim of relativism—claiming there are no objective truths, for all truths are relative—is true, for in the world of relativism there is no such thing as absolute truth. So our question should be: "Is that very claim objectively true?" If the answer is yes—yes, it is an objective truth—then the claim leads to contradiction: if the claim is true, it becomes false. This issue has become known from the famous Liar Paradox: Epimenides, a Cretan, says "All Cretans are liars." Is Epimenides telling the truth or is he not? If he is, he is not; if he is not, he is. Whatever answer we choose, we are led into contradiction. And contradictions are a serious warning sign that there is something wrong with what we are saying.

Not surprisingly, relativists have tried to prove that relativism does *not* contradict itself. Their strategy is to argue that no universal statement can ever refer to itself, so stating that all truth is relative supposedly cannot refer to this statement itself. These relativists received some support from the British philosopher Bertrand Russell, who tried to argue that nothing could logically refer to *itself* (called his "Theory of Logical Types"). Thus, relativism could be one of those cases where "self-reference" is not allowed. However, Russell's argument in itself is also a statement that defeats itself, since in presenting the Theory of Types, Russell can hardly avoid referring to the Theory of Types, which is doing something that he tells us can't be done or shouldn't be done. Why would the rule against self-reference be true? One need merely consider the word "word" and ask whether it refers to itself. Of course it does. The word "word" is a word. Excluding or forbidding self-reference is not a viable way to follow, not even to defend relativism.

Fourth, relativism typically reduces truth claims to a matter of neurological processes shaped by the process of evolution (see Chapter 14). Many evolutionary biologists think that we believe what we believe because what we think is "truth" actually emerges from brains shaped by natural selection. Evolutionary biologists argue that "not thinking straight" would be a disadvantage in the struggle for survival, and therefore would be selected against. At least, these scientists admit that natural selection itself is capable of capturing reality because it operates depending on the way the world "is." But that's where capturing reality ends for them. Yet, their argument sounds certainly attractive. No matter how attractive it sounds, it is not really adequate, for several reasons.

If truth were really the product of natural selection, we would run into several serious problems. One of them is that natural selection cannot operate on those truth claims that are not directly related to survival. As a matter of fact, many of the things we try to rationally understand are basically useless for survival, whereas illusions sometimes prove pretty useful. Indeed, not all truths and truth claims have survival value. Truth for truth's sake is anything but survival minded. The human intellect gives us the power to "understand" a wide variety of things that go far beyond mere survival. Knowing that the earth revolves around the sun, for instance, doesn't help us in the struggle for survival.

Another reason why natural selection cannot really explain truth is that truth trumps success in survival. True explanations may indeed be successful and useful, but successful or useful explanations are not necessarily true. Ptolemy's geocentrism, for instance, was successful and useful in navigation, but it wasn't true. So natural selection cannot always be the arbiter of what is true or false. What natural selection tests could perhaps be the *effectiveness* of knowledge, but not necessarily its *truthfulness*. As Alvin Plantinga puts it, "Natural selection is interested, not in truth, but in appropriate behavior." That makes quite a difference. If Ptolemy's geo-centrism and Copernicus's helio-centrism had to go through the filter of natural selection, either one would pass the test, but only rationality can help us decide which one is true.

Another reason why natural selection cannot explain all truths we know is the fact that certain thoughts—such as the thought that the number 11 is a prime number—are "necessarily" true. This kind of certainty is beyond the trial-and-error strategy of natural selection. So the question is how natural selection could produce the knowledge of such truths—for example, the knowledge that the laws of logic and mathematics are without any exceptions. Do those who believe that the number 11 is a prime number really have a better chance of surviving than those who do not believe this? That's hard to accept. How could natural selection ever produce in us the knowledge that the laws of logic are universally valid and allow for no exceptions? That cannot be a matter of trial and error in the "battle for survival."

Then there is even a more serious problem for natural selection as being the source of truths. When biologists claim that our beliefs are mere artifacts, such a claim would act like a boomerang that destroys its own truth claims. They undermine their own truth claims by cutting off the very branch that the biologists who make such claims are—or actually were—sitting on. That makes for a self-destructive claim.

It is hard to see, for instance, how Newton's discovery of gravity, Mendel's discovery of genes, and Darwin's discovery of natural selection could have been catapulted by genes that had gone through the process of natural selection. "Eureka's" don't come from genes nor from natural selection. Their "sudden" discovery was not the result of a survival strategy or a mutation in genes. So we must come to the conclusion that attempts of evolutionary biologists to reduce human knowledge to a product of genes and natural selection are doomed to fail. What remains standing is that the human mind does have direct access to reality and to the world of truths and untruths. We can make mistakes of course, but we can find out why we do. We have the capacity to capture the truth of the way things *are*—although this may often be a challenging process with many hurdles.

Some side effects of Relativism

As mentioned already, relativism has had an impact on various areas, in particular on science and religion. Let's study in more detail its impact on these two domains separately.

One of the side effects of relativism can be seen in science—at least in some new interpretations of scientific results and theories. Once the road of science is presented as an essentially disconnected succession of paradigms, like Thomas Kuhn had suggested, science has become another victim of relativism. However, the truth of the matter is that even Kuhn had to admit that "the world remains the same even after it is seen in a totally different perspective following the paradigm shift." In other words, it is reality that connects different paradigms.

Compare this with different languages: beneath the different words of different languages you find common concepts—and this is what makes translation from one language to another possible. Ironically, Kuhn's relativism makes each paradigm absolute and, as he calls it, "incommensurable" with other paradigms—its own authority in matters of truth, so to speak. The late physicist Fr. Stanley Jaki rightly remarks, "Indeed, no great scientist has ever hoped to make a discovery incommensurable with all that had previously been discovered in science." Instead, there is a continuous process in science to search for, and to come closer and closer to, objective truth—maybe sometimes with revolutionary leaps—as long as reality demands it.

Why does science still hold on to its truth claims against claims of relativism? Well, if truth were at the mercy of some individual scientists, science would have to abandon all its universal claims. In fact, it is reality that sometimes forces scientists to revise their theories, or even their professed paradigms, in order to capture the truth better. They constantly need to adjust the "speculations" in their minds to the "hard data" of reality. No wonder, the much heralded idea of falsification says that a theory is in trouble when its predictions turn out to be false—that is, not-true. This takes us back again to the age-old philosophical idea of absolute, objective truth.

All scientists tacitly assume in their actions the objectivity of nature and the ability of the mind to grasp it ever more comprehensively. Relativism would be detrimental to their pursuit. There is nothing wrong with looking at scientists and their searching for truth from a psychological, socio-logical, or historical perspective, but truth itself is not a psychological, sociological, or historical issue. Truth is truth, even if you do not accept it; and untruth is untruth, even if you claim it. Truth is truth—for everyone, anywhere, at any time. In other words, it needs to be stressed that we do not create truth, like artists and artisans do; we do not reach truth by consensus but by discovery, which is in fact what scientists and explorers try to do. Our perception of truth, our understanding of it, and our commitment to it may vary according to the state of art in science or philosophy. But truth itself doesn't change.

Even science itself cannot reduce questions about truth to matters of genes or natural selection. One cannot have it both ways. If you accept the objectivity and truthfulness of your biological knowledge, including your evolutionary theories, you cannot come to the conclusion that evolutionary theory, in turn, teaches us that all human knowledge is just a relative issue—a mere product of genes selected during evolution. To claim that the theory of natural selection is a matter of truth, and at the same time, that truth is supposedly the product of natural selection makes for a "boomerang theory" that undermines its own claims—once we consider it to be true, it becomes false. If I believe that my beliefs are determined by genes, then this very belief must also be determined by genes—which creates a paradox by violating the principle of non-contradiction. Consequently, the theory of natural selection cannot be the product of natural selection itself (see Chapter 14).

Let's move on now from the scientific realm to the religious realm. Does religion have anything to do with truth? Of course it does, regardless of claims to the contrary by those relativists who consider religion a matter of mere opinions, feelings, and emotions. God's existence is a factual matter—God either exists or does not exist. Believing that God does not exist does not make him disappear, as little as believing that the earth is flat would make the earth flat. Frank Cronin of Aquinas College expresses this as follows: "If it turns out God doesn't exist, it isn't that our faith was wrong—our facts were wrong.... Our faith is wrong because we got the facts wrong." Perhaps it is safer to say, not that our facts were wrong, but that our facts were not facts but fiction.

Apparently, even in religion, we deal with facts and truth issues. What Catholicism claims is about truth—not just about personal, private feelings but about facts and truths as stated, for instance, in a Creed: "I believe in...." Jesus' resurrection is either true or false. God's coming again to judge the living and the dead is either true or false. Likewise, the existence of God is a factual issue that is either true or false. To put it more directly, God's existence is not dependent on our belief in him. God either exists or he doesn't—that's not a matter of opinion or feeling. You can have your own opinions and feelings, but you can't have your own facts. If Heaven doesn't exist, your belief in it doesn't make heaven spring into existence.

This also means, of course, that there are facts and truths other than scientific facts and truths. However, they may be of a different nature. They differ, for instance, in the way we get to those truths. As a result, science and religion convey two different kinds of truth—let's call them natural truths versus supernatural truths. The distinction of natural truths, which we gain through observation and experiment, versus supernatural truths, which we gain through revelation and faith, has quite some consequences. Science has *theories* to help our understanding, but they are subject to change, because we keep trying to capture the truth more and more, better and better. So let us not make science more than what it is—a work in progress. Religion, on the other hand, has *dogmas* to help our understanding, but they were revealed to us and therefore never change—so let us not make religion less than what it is. Science masquerading as religion is as unseemly as religion masquerading as science. Yet they both deal with truths and facts, no matter whether they are discovered or revealed.

What both kinds of truths have in common is this: truth is truth, even if you do not accept it; and untruth is untruth, even if you claim it. As much as it is a matter of fact that the earth is not flat—believing that it is flat does not make it flat—it is also a matter of fact that God exists—believing that he doesn't exist, does not make him disappear. Truth is truth, although we may not fully understand or capture the truth yet.

If there are indeed two kinds of truths—natural versus supernatural truths—we must ask ourselves whether they can be in conflict with each other. At the time of Thomas Aquinas, Islamic philosophers had introduced the idea that there can be "double truth." The concept of double truth meant that religious knowledge and philosophical knowledge may arrive at different, contradictory truths, but without detriment to either. By placing the "truths" of philosophy and science in one category and the "truths" of faith and religion in another, one could hold mutually exclusive positions as long as one believes that the opposing views are in separate departments of the mind—one for Sundays and one for weekdays, so to speak.

How would double truth be possible? In Islam, Allah could will one thing today and its opposite tomorrow. Allah's latest affirmation is always the binding one, but it can change the following day again, God willing. According to this view, since truth is not grounded in reasoning but in "willing," the only way we could know that the sun will arise in the morning is on condition that Allah wills it this morning and we believe it. Ultimately, this means that we cannot really rely on "nature" for anything. What is true today may not be true tomorrow.

Thomas Aquinas considered this view unsustainable. He saw with utter clarity that all truth comes from God, and therefore there can never be, ultimately, any conflict between the outcome of reason and the beliefs of faith, or between the data of the sciences and the facts of revelation, or between natural truths and supernatural truths. He claimed that faith and reason, or theology and philosophy, or science and religion, play, in his own words, "complementary roles in the quest for truth. Grace does not destroy nature but fulfills it." So we have to thank Thomas Aquinas, and the Catholic Church, for constantly reminding us that all truth is God's truth and is therefore universal, global, and permanent. God has revealed himself both in the Scriptures and in the natural world. Therefore, if we find a seeming contradiction between the two, we have not understood correctly either the Scriptures or the natural world, or both.

Perhaps a few examples may demonstrate how important the rejection of "double truth" is. Since there are truths of reason and observation as well as truths of faith and revelation—which can never contradict each other—it cannot be true that the earth is flat according to faith and religion, but at the same time spherical according to reason and science, for that would create a contradiction. In a similar way, if science tells us that the earth circles the sun, it cannot be true that the sun revolves the earth. In all such cases, and there are so many others, we are dealing with contradictions which cannot be both true at the same time given the fact that there is no "double truth." When we detect a "double truth," either one or both must have been claimed in error and must be reevaluated.

One word of caution, though. Sometimes we might think we have a double-truth issue, when in fact we do not. For instance, creation as understood by faith versus the Big Bang theory as understood by science do not contradict each other. The Big Bang theory is about the *beginning* of the universe—about how physical interactions came about— whereas faith in creation is about the *origin* of the universe— about where the Universe came from and how it completely depends on God for its existence. Here is another example: Creation, as understood by faith, versus evolution, as understood by science, do not contradict each other. Creation is about how natural causes are related to God, whereas evolution deals with how natural causes are related to each other through processes such as reproduction and natural selection. The same can be said about randomness in science and Providence in faith. Randomness is about how events can be related to each other, whereas Providence is about how events are related to God. So we do not need to make a choice between two truths in these cases because there is no problem of "double truth" here.

Where does all of this leave us? Modern society has been tyrannized by the despotism of relativism, which arrogantly asserts that we have been born "blind" and that truth is beyond our reach. The best we can go for is personal opinions and private beliefs. As a consequence, most people think belief in absolute and objective truths is intolerant because it pretends to know "the" truth. Well, those who believe this can't claim either that they "possess" the truth of relativism; instead, they must "listen" obediently to the truth—and that's what both scientists and religious believers are supposed to do. If that's considered being intolerant, one could as well, or even better, make the case that relativism is actually the intolerant doctrine, because it conceitedly rejects any claim of truth as unacceptable. Indeed, intolerance can take on many faces. Relativists preach tolerance magnanimously, but only for those who agree with them—"my way or no way."

Let's come to a conclusion. Although we discussed several reasons for rejecting relativism, it keeps doing its devastating work in the minds of many. It is probably the basis of all the other doctrines we will discuss in the upcoming chapters. Relativism keeps sowing doubt and suspicion—no matter whether it is in science, in religion, or even in daily life. The French philosopher Jacques Maritain said it right, "The sole philosophy open to those who doubt the possibility of truth is absolute silence—even mental."

Given all of the above, we must come to the conclusion that relativism is a doctrine which is not only seriously flawed but also very destructive.

2. Syncretism

What is Syncretism?

Syncretism is the doctrine that different faiths and beliefs can best be combined into one comprehensive, blended faith, especially in matters of religion. The main reason for promoting this doctrine is the fact that there are so many different religions that they might complement and enhance each other better when combined. For this reason, syncretism is considered a viable, even desirable option, superior to any of the individual faiths on their own. Syncretism is a plea for a thoroughly inclusive approach of all religious faiths.

How could syncretism become an attractive option for so many people? Probably the most convincing argument supporting this doctrine is the fact that there are so many religions with very different beliefs, and yet they all claim to own the final truth. This is often explained by assuming that all religions only have part of the truth—so perhaps combined they may have the whole truth. This seems to call for syncretism.

To illustrate this position of syncretism, some use the ancient fable of six blind men who visit the palace of the Rajah in India and encounter an elephant for the first time. As each blind man touches the animal with his hands, each felt a different part of the elephant, announcing an elephant to be all trunk, all tail, etc. An argument ensued, each blind man thinking his own perception of the elephant was the correct one. Awakened by the commotion, the Rajah called out from the balcony, "The elephant is a big animal. Each man touched only one part. You must put all the parts together to find out what an elephant is like."

The message is clear: Each one had only found part of the truth. In an analogous way, the different truth claims of all religions must be equivalent to each other, for no one has the entire picture, just pieces of it. Ultimately, all religions are supposedly equal in being incomplete, or even inadequate. Had these people searched in a more inclusive and comprehensive way, and would they have listened to each other, they would have discovered they had only half-truths, not the full-truth. That's why we need syncretism, so the doctrine tells us. It pleads for an amalgam of various religions.

Another frequently heard argument used to support syncretism is that most religions worship the same God anyway—no matter whether they call God by the name of Yahweh, Allah, Brahman, Krishna, or you name it. The names for God may be different in different religions, but ultimately they must refer to the same person, God in Heaven. In other words, most religions do share the same truth: God—although they differ when they go into further "details" about God. For this reason, there is more that unites religions than what separates them. This is often called the idea of "common ground." It is based on the notion that if we abstract enough from particular beliefs about God, we will eventually arrive at some kind of "universal" God on whom we can all agree.

The "common ground" approach has been very popular and has been frequently used to promote "ecumenism" between Christian denominations, or even "interfaith dialogue" across an increasingly wide board, from Catholics to Protestants, from Christians to Jews and Muslims, from revealed religions to Buddhism and Hinduism, from monotheism to polytheism. Needless to say that syncretism has been a strong voice in a powerful plea for dialog between all religions on a global scale—some kind of global ecumenism.

In short, syncretism defends itself from two different angles. Put in a negative way, all religions on their own are inadequate. Put in a more positive way, all religions have a common ground between them. Either way leads to a need for blending religions.

What is wrong with Syncretism?

Probably the most serious problem of syncretism is that we ultimately could end up with a very abstract and stripped concept of God—something like "a god-within," a god we all are supposed to have in common in our inner selves. That's arguably the most extreme outcome of syncretism—leaving us with a religion in an empty shell. It degrades the notion of God into the "semi-religious" idea of "a god-within." Perhaps the best verdict on this outcome has been given by G.K. Chesterton when he said, "Of all horrible religions the most horrible is the worship of the god within.... That Jones shall worship the god within turns out ultimately to mean that Jones shall worship Jones." Thus we all have become divine.

But there are other problems with the doctrine of syncretism. First of all, the existence of so many different religions cannot be used as an argument against any religion in particular. G.K. Chesterton, again, was eager to debunk this argument with a simple analogy:

> *It is perpetually said that because there are*
> *a hundred religions claiming to be true, it is*

therefore impossible that one of them should really be true…. It would be as reasonable to say that because some people thought the earth was flat, and others (rather less incorrectly) imagined it was round, and because anybody is free to say that it is triangular or hexagonal, or a rhomboid, therefore it has no shape at all; or its shape can never be discovered.

Neither can the story of the king who saw the blind men and the elephant from his balcony be used as a call for syncretism. If we want to come to the conclusion that partial truths have to be combined into one comprehensive truth, we must have a full and accurate view of the entire picture—just as the king had from his balcony, looking at the blind men and the elephant. The Rajah was in a position of privileged access to the truth. Because he could see clearly, he was able to correct those who were blind. If everyone truly is blind, then no one can even know who is mistaken.

Only someone who knows the whole truth can identify another on the fringes of it. In this story, only the king can do so—no one else. The Christian apologist Greg Koukle words it correctly:

If the story-teller is like one of the six who can't see—if he is one of the blind men groping around—how does he know everyone else is blind and has only a portion of the truth? On the other hand, if he fancies himself in the position of the king, how is it that he alone escapes the illusion that blinds the rest of us?

So we must come to the conclusion that the idea of partial

truths is in the end indefensible. It's like saying, "Each one of us is blind," and then adding, "but I'll tell you what the world really looks like." That's a clear contradiction.

There is also a problem with the assumption of syncretism that all religions have a common ground in worshipping the same God. What is wrong with that? Well, it is in essence based on the distinction between *reference* and *description*. Yahweh and Allah, for instance, have the same reference—referring to the same God in Heaven—although their descriptions are rather different. There are other cases like that. Think of the following. You are probably familiar with the Evening Star—a rather bright object in the sky during a clear evening. Perhaps, as an early riser, you are also familiar with the Morning Star, a very prominent object that has attracted many people's attention in the early morning. For centuries, some people have admired the Evening Star, while others enjoyed the Morning Star. It turned out, however, that it is the same object they are talking about and admiring—the planet Venus, that is.

Something similar can be said about religion, at least according to the doctrine of syncretism. The argument of syncretism goes as follows: If, according to monotheism, there can only in principle be one God, then Christians, Jews, and Muslims must be worshipping the same God—the same reference in Heaven. Therefore, it does not matter which religion we choose to worship God. In analogy, whether you speak of the Morning Star or the Evening Star, you are ultimately speaking of the same thing, the planet Venus. That clearly seems to be a strong point of syncretism.

The problem with this argument is, however, that the same reference may come with very different descriptions. Aristotle's "sun," for instance, refers to the same sun as Galileo's "sun," but their descriptions are very different. The same can be said about the Morning Star, the Evening Star, and Venus: Although they refer to the same thing in the sky, they come with very different descriptions, which are not all worth the same. In calling this object in the sky "Venus," we have found a better designation for what people see at sunrise and what they see at sunset. Amazingly enough, the same thing can be seen at different moments, by different people, from different perspectives. No matter whether we say "Venus" or "Morning Star" or "Evening Star," we are talking about the same referent in the sky; and yet, the designation "Venus" is much more comprehensive and adequate than "Morning Star" or "Evening Star." We can't just declare them all equivalent.

Something similar can be said about religions. Even if it were true that many religions, at least the monotheistic ones, worship the same God, this does not mean their descriptions of God are the same. Their reference may be the same but certainly not their descriptions. The "common ground approach" of syncretism easily misses some essential differences between religions. Monotheistic religions may refer to the same God—in an abstract sense, that is—but the way they talk about this common reference is very different.

How can the God Muslims adore, for instance, be the same as the God Christians worship? Yes, they both talk about "love of God and neighbor," but for Muslims this extends only to other Muslims. The Muslim God, Allah, commands to kill or subjugate Jews and Christians, unless they accept the God of Islam. Besides, Allah curses anyone who says that God has a son. Allah allows, or even promotes, a morality of polygamy, marrying six-year old girls, harsh punishments, and holy wars. The Muslim heaven is a man's haven where each man is rewarded with 72 beautiful, high-bosomed virgins—a place so totally different from the Christian heaven where the bliss comes from the pure joy of being in God's presence. And, what is more, it is hard to deny that Sharia law in Islam is fundamentally different from social justice in Christianity.

Are these just details that do not matter? Even if there is much common ground between Muslims and Christians, some might suggest not to advertise it, as it would entitle atheists to portray Christianity and Islam as "evil twin brothers." As a result, the common ground begins to look more like thin ice. As the title of a recent book poses the question, "Is the Father of Jesus the God of Mohammed?" Or are they perhaps essentially different? Even the Qur'an itself suggests that the God of the Qur'an is radically different from the God Christians worship. The Qur'an specifically tells us that Christ was not divine, was not crucified, and that speaking of the Trinity is a form of polytheism. To affirm these Christian teachings constitutes blasphemy for Muslims. Their religion, in short, is considered very different from other religions. So we need to keep in mind that different religions entertain very different descriptions of God.

But in addition, one might even question whether the monotheistic religions really share the same *reference*. Let me use the example of Venus again: "Venus" may be the same referent behind "Morning Star" and "Evening Star," but there is much more to it. Talking about "Venus" may refer to very different entities: for some it refers to a planet, for some to a Greek goddess, for others to a horoscope—which are not only different descriptions but also very different references. In this view, the difference between Yahweh and Allah would be more like the difference between Yahweh and Baal. Baal is a god, but not the God of Israel. The Old Testament makes very often a distinction between God, on the one hand, and gods, idols, or demons, on the other hand. Only Yahweh is God, but all the other gods are not God but rather God's creations which rebelled against him and became fallen spirits. Let's leave it at that.

Some side effects of Syncretism

Once we assume that most religions are united by having the same reference—as the "common ground" approach of syncretism does—it becomes very tempting to also assume that differences in the description of God are all of the same quality. Even if many religions have the same reference, God, this does not entitle us to conclude that all religious conceptions of God are worth the same.

In other words, not all religions are of the same quality. For instance, religions are definitely not equal, let alone equivalent, in the sense of all being true, as there are obvious contradictions between them. If the descriptions of God in different religions are in contradiction with each other, then they cannot all be true at the same time (see Chapter 1). Judaism and Islam, for instance, teach their followers that Jesus is not the Son of God, whereas Christianity teaches he is. Well, Jesus either is the Son of God or he's not. These two claims can't both be right. The notion that Christianity and Judaism are equally true is contradictory, in the same way as a "square circle" is. Contradictory claims can't be simultaneously true. Another example is the fact that the Qur'an denies the Trinity, the Divinity of Jesus, and even his Crucifixion, which are essential to most of Christianity. They cannot be both true at the same time. When religions contradict each other, then at least one of them must be false—which makes for a much divided pantheon. So the acclaimed equality of religions seems to float on thin air.

And then there are the differences the Christian religion has with Hinduism and Buddhism. Since Buddha deliberately avoided talking about the existence or non-existence of God, it is obvious that Buddhists will have difficulty when faced with the Christian belief in Jesus as the Son of God, true God and true man. Besides, by ignoring God and by making salvation rest solely on personal effort, Buddha substituted for the Brahmin religion a cold and colorless system of philosophy that has no place for God, not to mention for Jesus, the Son of God.

Something similar holds for Hinduists. As the Vatican Commission for Interreligious Dialogue put it in 2000, "Many Hindus have no difficulty in accepting Jesus as divine. What they find difficult is the Christian understanding that the Incarnation of God in Jesus is unique. Jesus is often seen as the supreme example of self-realization, the goal of the Hindi dharma. He is taken to be a symbol of human progress. For some he becomes more of an ideal than a historical person."

Hence we must come to the conclusion that religions are definitely not equal in the sense of all being true, as there are obvious contradictions between them. We have to decide which description is true. There must be more to it than having the same reference. What then can help us decide whether a religion is true or not?

The fact that a religion claims to be true doesn't make that religion true. Think of this: When defendants in court plead innocent, does that mean they are in fact innocent? Just claiming innocence does not validate one's innocence. Similarly, when religions claim to be true, that does not make them true. Some religions are so "weird" that they could never even qualify to be true. What about the Church of the Flying Spaghetti Monster, to name just one extreme case? In 2016, even a federal judge in the USA ruled that this church is not a real religion—let alone a true religion.

Not all "religious beliefs" have a claim to our respect—we must respect their members, and perhaps even their beliefs, but not necessarily their truth claims. This might eliminate quite a few of them. Questionable candidates would be, for instance, the Branch Davidians, Nuwaubianism, the Scientology Church, the Nation of Yahweh, the Unification Church, the white supremacist World Church of the Creator, and the list keeps growing. Recently, in the name of "freedom of religion," courts allowed after-school programs for Satanism, which is not even a religion but an anti-religion. And what about humanism (see 5), which is taught as a form of religion in some public schools?

In other words, we need at least one important deciding factor to determine which beliefs are true, and which are not. There are strong arguments to make *reason* this deciding factor (see Chapter 1). Reason is our most important tool to decide what is true and what is false—not only in science but also in religion. Religious beliefs that are against reason cannot be true; religious faith that is not open to reason cannot be true; religions that are irrational and incoherent cannot be true; contradictions between religions cannot be accepted. In fact, reason is the best, if not only, interreligious criterion to judge a religion's truth. As said earlier, not all religions are created equal. Pope Benedict XVI even spoke of "sick and distorted forms of religion." Religions based on extraterrestrial sources or on books that only some people are supposed to have access to or on books that no longer exist have a hard time to pass the test of reason. Not all "religious beliefs" qualify as a legitimate form of religion, unless they pass at least the test of reason. The fact that someone believes in UFO religions, also referred to as "UFO cults" or "flying saucer cults," does not automatically authenticate them as a true religion.

In other words, not everything that calls itself religion may be regarded a legitimate religion. The canons of reason are needed to weed out what is plausible or implausible in whatever a certain religion tells us about God, for not all religious beliefs are of the same quality. Only religious beliefs that convey truth are of the right quality. *Truth* is the keyword here, together with that other related keyword, *reason*. Truth can't be against reason. If a certain belief is irrational or unreasonable, then it can't be true, for truth is more than what we believe to be true. A belief in square circles can't be true. A counter-factual belief can't be true: If the earth is round or spherical, my belief cannot make it flat. You can have your own beliefs, but you cannot have your own facts. Facts are based on truth and reason, even in religion—otherwise they are illusions.

The Catholic Church is arguably unique in Christianity, and even among other religions, for so strongly advancing the role of reason and truth in religion. She does not accept beliefs that go against reason or are otherwise unreasonable. She is actually known for her motto "Faith *and* Reason" [*Fides et Ratio*]. It is her deepest belief that reason comes from God as much so as faith does. In his 1998 encyclical *Fides et Ratio*, John Paul II warned of "a resurgence of fideism, which fails to recognize the importance of rational knowledge and philosophical discourse for the understanding of faith, indeed for the very possibility of belief in God."

This perspective on reason has a long history in the Catholic Church. As it was said about St. Paul, "He entered the synagogue, and for three months debated boldly with persuasive arguments about the Kingdom of God" (Acts 19:8). Apparently, even religious faith is something we can reason, argue, and debate about. Soon after, St. Augustine could not have said it more clearly, "Believers are also thinkers: in believing, they think and in thinking, they believe." He also introduced his two famous formulas (ca. 400) which express the coherent synthesis between faith and reason: "Believe in order to understand" [*Crede ut intel-*

ligas], but also, and inseparably, "Understand in order to believe" [*intellige ut credas*]. The same idea can also be found in St. Anselm's two famous phrases (11th century), "Faith seeking understanding" and "I believe in order that I might understand." In other words, in order to find God and believe, you must scrutinize truth *and* reason. So it should not surprise us then that the Catholic Church also follows St. Thomas Aquinas, a Doctor of the Church, in defending the principle that faith cannot be against reason. When something is against reason, God cannot endorse it, let alone create it.

So we may conclude that Catholicism is arguably the most rational and coherent of all religions. When it comes to faith, Catholics are encouraged to use their heads. They don't believe that religious faith is immune to rational argumentation and scrutiny by reason. Catholics are thinkers: in believing they think, and in thinking they believe. This reciprocal relationship between faith and reason has been a constant theme in Catholic intellectual history, and it explains why the Catholic intellectual tradition is so rich, strong, and full, perhaps unlike any other religion in the world. In his famous Regensburg address and elsewhere, Pope Benedict XVI stressed the perennial relevance of Pope John Paul II's encyclical *Fides et Ratio* (Faith and Reason) and the need for Faith to purify Reason, and for Reason to purify Faith.

This explains why *apologetics* is so pivotal in Christianity. What it does is defending the faith with rational arguments. Apologetics tries to present a rational basis for the Catholic Faith and to defend it against objections. Apologetics is actually an important activity in the history of the Church. Its goal is to show how reasonable faith is, or at least to demonstrate that faith is not against reason. If there are no rational arguments for a certain religious belief, we should seriously question the truth of such a belief. This makes reason the common ground between believers and non-believers, so it is an important apologetic tool.

Based on what we have said so far about faith and reason, Catholicism has the right to claim it is the only religion with the full truth about God. But she adds to this that other religions "often reflect a ray of that truth which enlightens all men" (Vatican II, *Nostra aetate*, n. 2). Other religions possess some aspect of the truth, with varying degrees of clarity. But only the Catholic Church possesses the fullness of the truth, the fullness of God's revelation. Rabbi Israel Zolli, the Chief Rabbi of Rome during Nazi occupation, who converted to Catholicism after World War II, explained why he chose the Catholic, rather than the Protestant, Church: "The Catholic Church was recognized by the whole Christian world as the true Church of God for fifteen consecutive centuries. No one can halt at the end of those 1,500 years and say that the Catholic Church is not the Church of Christ without embarrassing himself seriously." C.S. Lewis beautifully summarized this, "I believe in Christianity as I believe that the sun has risen: not only because I see it, but because by it I see everything else."

Does this mean that any kind of dialogue with other religions is out of the question? Certainly not, but we do have to put it in the right perspective. Any kind of dialogue between religions must be honest about the differences that separate them—sparing us a false impression of "common ground," for God is also "in the details." All dialogue should come to the truth, but with respect and love. Pope Benedict's encyclical *Charity in Truth* articulates very well that the aim of any religious dialogue is ultimately truth. We can and should agree to agreeably disagree. If Christians believe—as they do—that Jesus Christ is God's all-inclusive revelation, then there can be no correction or addition to it.

Obviously, respect for other religions does not mean we have to let go of any truth claims—so we don't have to go along to get along. Those who think otherwise wrongly identify respect for people with respect for beliefs. Benedict XVI was right when he expressed a deep respect for Muslims, but that is not the same as having a deep respect for Islam. The 2011 interreligious prayer meeting in Assisi made unmistakably clear that gathering together to pray is not the same as praying together, for praying together implies that we are believing in the same God and are praying to the same God—which may not be the case. On the other hand, people from different religions, although they may have very different understandings of the divine, should come together to pray at the same time for the same intention—their longing for peace—even though they cannot pray together to the same God.

Given all of the above, we must come to the conclusion that syncretism is a doctrine which is not only seriously flawed but also very destructive.

3. Gnosticism

What is Gnosticism?

Many people may have never heard of Gnosticism; to others, it is probably best known from early Church history. However, there is much more to it than what it is portrayed to be. On the one hand, Gnosticism is undoubtedly much older than early Christianity, when it was at its highest peak. On the other hand, Gnosticism has remained very much alive even after its climax—now even more than ever.

Gnosticism is a complex phenomenon that incorporates several, rather diverse philosophies and beliefs. It is so complex and has so many different appearances that it is hard to characterize it in brief terms. But let us focus on some core characteristics.

The main element of Gnosticism is a deeply rooted *dualism*. First there is a dualism in god(s): a distinction between the unknowable god in heaven and the knowable god who created the world. The knowable god is the creator of the world, while the unknowable god is too transcendent to be directly involved with the creation. Gnosticism separates the demiurgic "creator" of the material world from the highest, unknowable god, who is an undefined infinite something, but not a personal being—rather, like Tad or Brahma of the Hindus, or the "Great Unknown" in modern thought.

Then Gnosticism declares a dualism in the world(s): the spiritual world versus the material world. This is connected with another dualism: the dualism of good and evil. The material world was created by an evil demi-god. The evil material universe is therefore at odds with the goodness of the spiritual world. The material world is not seen as something "good" but rather as a horrible mistake, created by a lower spiritual being, the "Demiurge." In other words, Gnostics hold that the world is flawed because it was created in a flawed manner.

The way Gnostics think about the world has profound consequences for the way they think about human beings. Because Gnostics recognize a sharp contrast between the inferior, finite world of matter and the transcendent, spiritual realm of the divine, they also have an understanding of the human being that sharply divides the material or bodily part, on the one hand, and the spiritual or mental part, on the other. For Gnostics, it is the immaterial—the spiritual and mental—that ultimately counts. They understand humans to represent sparks of the divine, but imprisoned in material bodies. Since matter and spirit are utterly opposed, the spirit needs to be freed from the body and return to its heavenly home. This redemption is only possible through gnosis—the Greek word for "knowledge"—which supposedly brings us "enlightenment" and the liberating knowledge of who we really are.

Based on this "gnosis," Gnosticism creates a condescending separation between the Gnostics and the masses. Gnostics consider themselves blessed with the real "gnosis" that everyone else lacks. Those who have attained higher levels of spiritual "knowing" and whose ascetic practices have refined their bodies into perfect temples of "the spirit," form an "elite" who can look with a sad disdain at those who are still tied to bodies and matter. Gnostics are "people who know," and their knowledge at once makes them a superior class of beings, whose present and future status is essentially different from that of those who, for whatever reason, do not know.

Where did such ideas and beliefs come from? Although Gnosticism was rather popular in the early centuries of Christianity, its roots are much older. Some scholars still bicker over where and when it first arose, but most now agree it had its origins in the ancient religion of Zoroastrianism, which originated more than six centuries ago in Persia. Though not a major religion anywhere in the world today, Zoroastrianism still has some adherents, mostly Indians in and around the city of Bombay who call themselves Parsees. Also, some Zoroastrians remain in the north of modern Iran. There is a group of them who claim to be tending a sacred fire in one of their temples that was originally lit thousands of years ago by their supposed founder, Zoroaster (also known as Zarathustra).

What defines Zoroastrianism is not so much its fire worship, but its dualism. It holds the gnostic belief that there are really two gods, not one. There is a good or benevolent god whose domain is of pure spirit. The other god, who is malevolent, is the one who created the material world. This makes everything material intrinsically evil. A person finds salvation by freeing himself from the desires and even legitimate demands of the flesh.

The Roman Empire was a fertile soil for such gnostic beliefs. In times of uncertainty and gloominess, people often look for something new and exciting. And lo and behold, something new was brewing in the empire: a mixture of ideas drawn from Persia, ancient Oriental religions, Greek philosophy, sorcery, and other mysterious cults. This potion became known as Gnosticism. It was an eclectic movement generated out of a general experience of profound malaise in a dying culture. Gnosticism was not an organized religion but it rather offered a general way of thinking and believing for those in crisis.

Gnosticism did not die when Christianity came along. It remained a popular belief, but now outfitted with more specific details by incorporating some semi-Christian elements. It used some Christian terminology but with a completely different meaning. We could briefly summarize its new disguise as follows.

1. Matter is evil, so one can do with one's body whatever one wants, including killing it to release the soul from its imprisonment.

2. People are saved by acquiring secret knowledge, gnosis, which is imparted only to the initiated.

3. The God of the Old Testament is evil, as evidenced by the fact that he created the material universe. He is different from the God of the New Testament, who is the God of Love, as Jesus and his apostles taught.

4. Jesus Christ was not truly God, the second Person of the Trinity, for he was merely a created being who was the lowest of a group of semi-divine beings between God and man.

5. Although Jesus Christ appeared to be human, his humanity was merely an illusion.

6. Christ only appeared to die, but did not really die, so the Crucifixion was in fact a cruci-fiction.

7. Jesus gave his disciples some secret information that cannot be found in the Bible.

Ideas like these would also blossom in another, later movement, Manicheanism. Its founder, Mani, born in Persia, asserted in the third century AD that, to avoid being corrupted by Creation's evil, human beings should refuse to work or fight, as well as refuse to marry. The radicalism of Mani's teaching—widespread acceptance of it would make life in society impossible—led to his execution, but by the end of that century his ideas, which we know as Manicheanism, had spread to the Roman Empire. Even St. Augustine fell victim to it for a short period of time.

Once expelled from Rome and Milan, Manichaeism would stay dormant for a long time, and finally came back in a new disguise, Catharism. Catharism was a blend of Gnosticism and Manichaeism. From this, Catharists drew two different conclusions: Some believed that the body needed to be destroyed by fasting and through other ascetic exercises; others believed that it didn't matter what you did with your body since only the soul matters. Not only were the beliefs of Catharism heretical, they also entailed serious social consequences, detrimental to civilization. Marriage was scorned because it legitimized sexual relations, which Catharists identified as the Original Sin. But fornication was permitted because it was temporary, secret, and was not generally approved of, whereas marriage was permanent, open, and publicly sanctioned. The ramifications of such theories are not hard to imagine. Ritualistic suicide was encouraged, and Catharists refused to take any oaths and opposed all governmental authority.

Although Gnosticism may seem an old doctrine and heresy, something of the past, it is still very much alive in our modern times. We find it again in Jung's "depth psychology," although some elements in Jung's depth psychology are insightful, some elements certainly can be considered Gnosticism in contemporary guise. We find gnostic elements also in the occult "New Age" spirituality, and in movies and books such as *The Da Vinci Code*. Ideas like these are in essence modern versions of Gnosticism. They set the soul in opposition to the body, based on the gnostic belief that only the soul is considered the "real me," thus leaving the body at the mercy of the soul. All Gnostics, ancient and modern, believe that the soul is trapped in the body and needs to be freed from this dungeon. However, it can only be freed by learning secret knowledge. This is certainly a gnostic idea that can still be heard frequently in modern Western culture.

What is wrong with Gnosticism?

How Gnostics know all of the above is a complete riddle. Their beliefs are an amalgam of various philosophies, doctrines, ideas, beliefs, and what have you. Yet they know all of this because they just know and have the right "gnosis." Which sounds very much like a form of self-refuting, circular reasoning: they know what they know because they just know. That creates a "building without a door"—there is no way to get in or out. There is no way to get from opinions to truths. There is no room for the test of reason. But there is much more to say against Gnosticism. Let's look at some details, starting with the dualism of gods.

When we talk about God, what do we mean? There are many possibilities, of course, but let us go back to the bare basics, to what practically all people could agree upon. We find these basics, for instance, with a very heterogeneous group of religious and non-religious thinkers such as Socrates, Plato, Aristotle, and Thomas Aquinas—to name just a few. Somehow, they all try to address the same fundamental question: How can this world help us to get to God?

Everyone will probably agree with the following starting point. All things can cause *other* things to change but they cannot be the cause of their *own* existence. You cannot be your own parent, for instance. Or, you cannot give your own existence to yourself or receive it from yourself. This explains, for example, that children need parents—which makes for a long chain or sequence of generations. Theoretically, this sequence can go back far in time, even infinitely far back in time. That would be an example of infinite regress. Although infinite regress is perfectly acceptable in mathematics—negative numbers go on to infinity just as positive numbers do—it is not acceptable when it comes to real beings. Real beings are not like numbers: they need causes. Even if we use mirrors to project an image into infinity, that's not really infinity but merely an optical illusion of infinity.

However, infinite causation going infinitely back in time does not really explain anything. Although each son's existence is caused by his father (and mother, of course), the cause of that father must go back in time in an infinite way without ever finding a "first father" in the link of fathers— and therefore, it goes back in time without ever finding a real cause or explanation. And even if we do find a "first father," where then does this father come from, for he cannot generate himself? Besides, even if infinite causation would explain something, it certainly does not explain everything about fathers and sons, for the question remains: what is it that enables fathers to generate sons at all? Where does that generation power come from? Moreover, a sequence of events in time may be able to go infinitely forward through the future and back through the past, but the problem would still be that we are dealing here with *time*, which in itself must have some other form of cause.

As Edward Feser puts it, an infinite series of causes can no more get you a real something than an infinite series of IOUs can give you real money—at some point, these IOUs have to be backed up by real money. In other words, the chain of causes needs to be hooked on to something else, so it doesn't hang from nowhere or just float in the air. Put differently, what is it that keeps this sequence or chain of causes going? There must be an ultimate cause—at a higher level—that explains all other causes. This led Thomas Aquinas to speak of a *Primary Cause* that explains all other, so-called secondary causes. Without a First Cause, none of the secondary causes could exist, let alone become causes of their own.

However, don't take the Primary Cause as the first one in a *temporal* sequence of causes. Instead we should be thinking in terms of an *explanatory* sequence of causes. To explain this difference, I will use the example of a book sitting on a bookshelf. Captured in a temporal sequence— let's call it a "horizontal" sequence—we could say the book was written by an author, and the author was the son or daughter of two parents, who were each, in turn, generated by other parents, etc.—with each step in the sequence going further back in time. Let's call this a "horizontal" sequence. Although there is a first parent in this particular example, that is not necessarily so. In theory, the chain could go back in time infinitely.

An explanatory sequence, on the other hand, would be very different. Let's call it a "vertical" sequence. I does not follow a time line but goes to a deeper and deeper level of explanation. To explain this concept, I would like to use the book again that is sitting on someone's bookshelf. The book has no capacity on its own to be five feet from the floor; it will be there only if something else, such as my book case, holds it up. But the book case in turn has no power of its own to hold the book there. It too would fall to the earth unless the floor held it aloft. And the floor, for that matter, could hold up the book case only because it is itself being held up by the house's foundation, and that foundation, in turn, by the earth, and the earth by the structure of the universe. All these "intermediaries" keep each other in tow. However, none of these things could hold up anything at all unless there were something which holds them up without having to be held up itself. That ultimate "something" is the Primary Cause. Without it, nothing in this series of causes would really be explained. This Primary Cause has the power to produce its effects without being caused by something else. It has *inherent* causal power while the secondary causes have only *derived* causal power.

The philosopher Michael Augros uses another analogy, the simple example of an I-beam with a hook on it from which a chain is to be hung: "If there is nothing for that whole chain to hang from, it will not hang, and nothing can be hung from it. There is nothing about those links in themselves that makes them want to hang in space.... There must also be something from which things hang and which is not itself hanging from anything." This is the "First Cause" or "Primary Cause" on whom everything in this Universe depends. All other causes are contingent—that is, not necessary and not self-explanatory. Even in case of an infinite series of contingent things, each caused by another one in the series, there is still the question of why the series itself exists at all, for the series is just as contingent as its individual contingent elements. That's where we need a necessary, self-explanatory, and uncaused Primary Cause to make all secondary causes possible. If we deny this, then we merely pass the explanatory "buck" rather than explaining anything.

Nothing less than such a necessary Being could possibly terminate the regress of explanation. This is obviously a chain that does not go back in time, instead it goes deeper and deeper. It is not a "horizontal" chain but a "vertical" chain. The Primary Cause must be "first" in a "vertical" way. It is a cause that exists eternally and explains any series of secondary causes. As St. Thomas Aquinas put it, "God is to all things the cause of being."

Therefore it has to be stressed that "First" should not be

taken as "first" in the sense of being before the second cause in time, and not "first" in the sense of coming before the second cause in a temporal sequence, but rather "first" in the sense of being the source of all secondary causes—a power from which all other causes derive their causal powers. In other words, the Primary Cause is not *temporarily* prior but *causally* prior to secondary causes. The Primary Cause must come "first" in the order of primacy (in a "vertical" sense), not in the order of time (in a "horizontal" sense).

I would say this is the most basic explanation of what we mean when we speak of God. What makes the Primary Cause so special is that it needs *no* cause. And what is so special about secondary causes is that they *do* need a cause, actually a Primary Cause. So the Primary Cause causes secondary causes to be causes of their own. This insight is based on common sense, without reference to any specific religion.

So this raises the question where Gnosticism goes wrong with its dualism of god(s). It is not possible that its two gods each enjoy perfectly independent self-existence. One of them must give being to the other, who then becomes the Primary Cause, or else they both derive their being from something else, which must then be the Primary Cause. However, in Gnosticism, the two gods—the good one and the bad one— are supposed to be quite independent from each other. They both existed from all eternity. Neither of them made the other, neither of them has any more right than the other to call itself god. One of them likes hatred and cruelty, the other likes love and mercy, and each backs its own view. That's where Gnosticism runs into trouble and therefore must be rejected as a false doctrine.

Let's move on to the dualism of world(s) in Gnosticism. Gnostics try to explain this world with its enigmatic mixture of good and evil by offering a solution to the question that has been troubling human minds for centuries: If God is good, why does he allow evil to exist, how can evil be part of his Creation? Gnosticism solves this problem by declaring that the world is flawed because it was created in a flawed manner by a flawed god. The Gnostics place a god who is the source of all good and everything spiritual versus a devil who is the source of all evil and everything material. For them, the good source and the evil source are equal in power and independent of each other.

However, the problem is that God, as the Primary Cause of the world, cannot be flawed and evil. God can only be all-good. We can say something positive about God based on what he created. We argue from the existence of secondary causes, which are familiar to us, to the existence of a Primary Cause who is unfamiliar to us. So we reason from finite secondary causes to an Infinite Primary Cause, from our finite imperfections to God's Infinite Perfections. Being the ultimate cause of our own existence, God must have all the perfections we find imperfectly in ourselves. For instance, God is all-perfect, all-powerful, and all-knowing, but also all-good. If there is evil in the world, it is not God's doing, but the doing of someone else, someone who cannot be the Primary Cause at the same time. In Christianity, this "someone else" is called Satan (see Chapter 11). Satan is certainly not a Primary Cause, but at best a secondary cause. Satan is not an adversary of God on the same level as God. Satan is considered to be a creature like you and me (although only spiritual), who has a free will like you and me (created in God's image and likeness), and who has decided to go against God. Satan is a fallen angel who has chosen to lead people into rebellion against God. Nevertheless, Satan is subordinate to God.

Let's move on next to the dualism Gnostics locate inside each one of us—it's a form of "body-self dualism." Gnostics, both ancient and modern, basically agree with Plato's philosophy, assuming two opposing forces working within humanity: flesh and spirit. In Plato's world, the spirit represents everything good and wholesome, while the flesh is everything evil and degenerative. Gnosticism took on this view and made it look like souls are trapped in dungeon-like bodies, and want to be released from their prison. However, such a separation between flesh and spirit, or between body and soul, is very questionable. One can separate body and soul in analysis but not in fact; we are body-soul composites. We can tell them apart but not set them apart. The fact that we distinguish body and soul does not entail that we can separate them, any more than the idea of a three-dimensional space means that we can separate those three dimensions. A body without a form, or soul, is a corpse; a soul without a body is what we call a ghost. There is no such thing as a disembodied soul or a soul-less human body. The body and the soul make for a "psycho-somatic" unity.

Yet, the gnostic idea that human beings are non-bodily persons inhabiting non-personal bodies never quite went away. It came back, for instance, when René Descartes compared our minds or souls with a pilot in his ship, suggesting that they pilot everything the body does. In this Cartesian view, a pilot can be without a ship, and a ship can be without a pilot. But it also implies that the "pilot" is in charge of the "ship" and can use it in whatever way he wants. This view was later dubbed a "ghost in the machine" kind of philosophy.

The Christian view of body-and-soul rejects the dualism of this "anti-body" heresy. Inspired by Aristotle and Thomas Aquinas, the soul is considered to be the substantial *form* of the body. In Aquinas' view, form and matter make up a substantial unity; one cannot have form without matter, nor matter without some form. Applied to the relationship between body and soul, this would indicate that the "form" of the soul gives a specific existence to the "matter" of the body. Body and soul, or spirit and flesh, are two sides of the same coin; the soul is the form of the body, or put differently, the spirit is the form of the flesh. In saying this, Aquinas embraces the total reality of the human person as an organic composite of spirit and matter, without emphasizing one element to the detriment of the other.

In this view, there is no human body without a human soul (unless it is a corpse), and there is no soul without a body (except temporarily, until the resurrection after death). A person is a unity of a human body and a human soul. So your body is an essential part of who you are—which is basically a common-sense idea. It's also the Christian message: When Jesus came to earth, he did not come to save us *from* the body but to save us *in* the body.

Then there is another strange element in Gnosticism: gnosis, the secret knowledge given only to the "initiated" and "educated" ones. Obviously, "secret" knowledge means that Gnostics can claim whatever they want, without the possibility of any further verification. They determine on their own what counts as knowledge. They do not subject their position, their beliefs, and their sources of authority to the sort of rigorous interrogation they want other believers to undergo. They are actually conceited and arrogant when they claim that they themselves know more than anyone else— which makes them invincibly ignorant.

No amount of contrary evidence or philosophical argument can convince someone who has private, direct, incorrigible, and impenetrable acquaintance with what they consider "The Truth." They just *know* what others do not know. Pope Francis gives us a timeless description of Gnosticism in his 2013 Apostolic Exhortation *Evangelii Gaudium* (#94): "a purely subjective faith whose only interest is a certain experience or a set of ideas and bits of information which are meant to console and enlighten, but which ultimately keep one imprisoned in his or her own thoughts and feelings."

Another questionable element of Gnosticism is its thinly disguised Pantheism. Pantheism states that "all is one, and everything is God." Thus it obscures the distinction between the Creator and his creation. It is exactly because the Creator is distinguished from his creation that God is divine and that his creation is not divine. All creatures totally depend on God for their existence. We are not God, nor are we gods ourselves. In contrast, without the real God, we would not even exist, and we certainly cannot make ourselves exist. God is active insofar as he creates the world, whereas the world is passive insofar as it received its existence from God. Denying this distinction is a very serious mistake. First we reasoned from secondary causes to the need of a Primary Cause, and then we destruct the very "ladder" from which we had climbed up to God.

The confused conception of pantheism leads easily to the idea of "a God within." It is Gnosticism when we hear that God is within us. The notion that God is "within" us in the sense that his divinity and power are also ours, and that this power makes all things possible to us—that, in effect, we are God—is in essence a gnostic distortion. Gnostic enlighten-ment is supposed to come from "knowing who I am," from "being in touch with my inner divinity", and from "becoming aware of my 'real' self." If the "real me" lies within, only I know who and what I am. You have to take my word for it—no one else can help me with that. In other words, the source of religious truth, for the Gnostic, lies within the individual, not outside it—not in history, tradition, or the community we live in, let alone in God.

All of the aforementioned flawed principles are at the core of Gnosticism. As to be expected, if these flawed basic principles are applied to Christianity, the outcome can only be flawed too. Christianity rejects every principle of Gnosticism, so there is no such thing as a gnostic version of Christianity—that's why Gnosticism is called a heresy. Catholics deem matter a valuable part of God's creation, whereas Gnostics consider all matter, including the body, as evil. In the Gnostic view, one can do anything one wants with one's body, including killing it to release the soul from its imprisonment. Catholics consider marriage and sex as gifts from God, whereas Gnostics deem them evil since their only purpose is making more "evil bodies." Catholics proclaim truth that is accessible to everyone, whereas Gnostics claim they have secret knowledge that is only accessible to the initiated. Catholics profess one God, all-good and all-powerful and all-knowing, who gradually revealed himself more and more in history, whereas Gnostics see the God of the Old Testament as an evil god who created the material universe and who is different from the God of the New Testament, who is the God of Love. Catholics adore Jesus Christ as God, as the second Person of the Trinity, whereas Gnostics see him as merely a created being who was the lowest of a group of semi-divine beings between God and man. Catholics see Jesus Christ as the God-Man who came to earth through the incarnation, whereas Gnostics consider it impossible for the "Word" to become "flesh," because spirit and matter are totally antagonistic. Whereas Catholics believe Jesus Christ really became man, who suffered and died for us, Gnostics regard his humanity and his crucifixion as merely an illusion, because they are embarrassed by Jesus' suffering and death. And there are many more differences between Christianity and Gnosticism. In short, the contrasts between the two could not be starker.

Some side effects of Gnosticism

It is very common nowadays to hear someone say, "I'm not religious, I'm spiritual." This is in fact a very Gnostic-esque statement. It comes with a smorgasbord of spiritual topics, ranging from "New Age," transcendentalism, astrology, reincarnation, and new ways of attaining "secret knowledge."

Such ideas are being promoted these days through books and the internet. That's not really a new phenomenon. Gnostics did something similar already ages ago when they tried to produce their own gnostic gospels which promoted new secret knowledge about Jesus. Their reasoning was that Jesus must have known that most Christians could not handle his true teaching, so he secretly entrusted it to a few elite confidants. Gnostics represent themselves as "improvers of the apostles," in the words of Irenaeus, a Church Father of that generation, who vehemently opposed the heresy of Gnosticism.

In their gnostic eyes, improvement was badly needed, for the apostles were just simple fisherman—plain, unlettered laborers who were unable to grasp fully the subtleties of their Teacher's message. The apostles whom Jesus had chosen were basically declared simpletons. Gnostics, however, were given "later and fuller" revelations passed down by Peter or Paul in secret. God had a secret, which was disclosed, but only in part, to certain "knowers"—the Gnostics. It is this secret knowledge that separates the initiated from the ignorant masses.

These gnostic groups composed their own writings, and labeled them with titles such as "The Gospel of Thomas" or "The Gospel of Philip" or "The Acts of Peter." They used Christian terminology and symbols, but placed them in an alien religious context that shattered the essential teachings of Christ. Of course none of these works can be traced to the apostolic times or apostolic authorship. The Gnostics shrewdly appended the names of the saints to these bogus writings only to give them more credibility, but they cannot be linked to the witness of an apostle or disciple, or their direct companions, which makes them heretical. Irenaeus interrogates the Gnostics directly: how could they have ever discovered more than the apostles? Little wonder the early Church condemned these writings.

The Church only accepted what was written by Christians who lived during the time of Christ and had known him personally or his direct witnesses. And they knew what these people had written and what they hadn't written. Based on this factual knowledge, the early Church established the canon of what should be part of the New Testament—and what should not. The genuine writings of the apostles (or their companions) made it into the Bible; all the other writings were excluded.

This is how we got our four gospels which are the "real Gospels." They were written by an apostle (Matthew, John) or an apostle's companion (Mark, Luke). These Gospels are orthodox in their teaching, particularly about the identity and person of Jesus. They were used in the Mass and other liturgical celebrations. Finally, they were accepted by the whole Church, not just by some sect. Evidence of the existence and use of these four Gospels is found already in St. Justin the Martyr's *First Apology* (c.150).

Present-day Gnostics use a strategy similar to what the ancient-day Gnostics did: they promote their insights and enlightenment by writing books that promote their Gnostic message under a semi-religious veil. G.K. Chesterton had it right, "Nine out of ten of what we call new ideas are simply old mistakes." A few brief examples of present-day Gnosticism may do.

One recent example is Scientology, which was launched in 1952 by L. Ron Hubbard. It basically promotes a form of Gnosticism that says salvation comes not through the saving actions of Jesus Christ but through the possession of special knowledge alone. Scientology claims that human beings are, in actuality, what they call "thetans," gods who have forgotten their god-like status. In contrast, the Catholic Church has always taught that we are, by nature, God's creatures and not gods in our own right. Because the Church of Scientology is based on secret knowledge and remains closed to outsiders, all of the claims made against it cannot be proven "beyond any doubt."

Another example is Dan Brown's popular book, *The Da Vinci Code*. It claims, among other things, that the apostles made Jesus into a god he never was and that therefore the biblical gospel cannot be trusted if you're interested in the "real Jesus." Numerous observers have been left scratching their heads as to why this book could become so successful. The "real Jesus," according to this novel, can only be known from the secret records which were secretly handed down to our age by the natural offspring of Jesus and Mary Magdalene. In other words, again we need "gnosis," which Dan Brown defines in his novel as "knowledge of the divine." Sounds familiar? *The Da Vinci Code* is thus no more than another form of Gnosticism, since its protagonists claim that the Gnostic gospels are, first of all, older than the biblical ones and, second, the only true records of Jesus' earthly life. All these claims are without any factual basis—only based on secret knowledge.

So we keep ending up with a modern version of Gnosticism, which teaches us that this world is a mere mirror image of the real world in heaven; that this world was created by an inferior, evil angel; that this world is bad; that souls are trapped in dungeon-like bodies; that souls can go through reincarnation; that God is a spirit we can find within; that Jesus is at best the heavenly teacher who brings to the "happy few" his saving and secret knowledge through gnostic intermediaries. That's how we can find the "the-god-within"—so we can say to ourselves, "I'm not religious, I'm spiritual."

Given all of the above, we must come to the conclusion that Gnosticism is a doctrine which is not only seriously flawed but also very destructive.

4. Secularism

What is Secularism?

Secularism is often understood as the principle of the separation of Church and State—separating religious institutions and religious dignitaries from government institutions and persons representing the state. Originally, the reason behind this separation of Church and State was to guarantee the free exercise of religion. This was done in reaction to situations in which the religion of the individual was made dependent almost totally upon the society into which one was born. Separating the Church from the State would give every citizen the right to choose whatever religion—or lack of religion—one wishes to choose, without any interference of the State. We could summarize this idea as "freedom *of* religion." It aims at protecting Religion from the State.

But gradually secularism has undergone a shift of focus. It became the view that public activities and decisions, especially political ones, should not be influenced by religious beliefs or practices. It came to be understood as a principle that aims not at protecting the Church from the State, but reversed, at protecting the State from Religion. In this altered sense, it wants a state or country to be free from religious rules and teachings, and to be entirely neutral on matters of belief. We could summarize this as "freedom *from* religion." At the present time, the term secularism is mostly, or almost exclusively, understood in its later, second sense: protecting the State from Religion—freedom *from* religion.

Where did such ideas come from? Secularism draws its intellectual roots from Greek and Roman philosophers such as Epicurus and Marcus Aurelius; but also from Enlightenment thinkers such as John Locke, Voltaire, James Madison, and Thomas Jefferson; and more recently, from freethinkers and atheists such as Bertrand Russell and Christopher Hitchens.

The term secularism itself, in its latest interpretation, originated in the mid-19th Century in the works of George Holyoake, a British newspaper editor, and his fellow atheists. It is in works such as his that the current usage was adopted in which "secular" is viewed as "free *from* religion." It has an anti-religious overtone—a vision of the future as devoid of religion, instead of separated from religion. It seeks to eliminate religion, or at the very least to privatize and thus marginalize it. Not only do these secularists take no interest at all in religious questions, but they even consider them completely irrelevant. In doing so, secularism reveals itself as a totalitarian doctrine, for it allows no room in the public square for anything but itself. It discards any religious views of the nature of the universe, or of the role of humanity in it. At best, it tolerates religion, while defending its own secular "values."

In spite of their seeming tolerance, secularists want only their own views and "values" to be taught and allowed in public life. The word "value" has become a code word for whatever secularists deem important in life. As with most fundamentalists and ideologues, they cannot give any rational justification for their views—they just assume their own views and values are right, and anyone who disagrees must be dealt with. This kind of secularism has in fact become extremely intolerant—that is, inclusive to everything but religion.

What is wrong with Secularism?

Pope John Paul II used to make a distinction between secularism and secularity. It is indeed an important distinction that will help us better understand what is happening in our modern, secularist society. Unlike secularism, secularity merely draws a dividing line between religion and state, or between religious institutions and governmental institutions.

Interestingly enough, this dividing line drawn between the Church and the State is a Christian invention—to be more precise, Jesus' own "invention." When Pope Benedict XVI discussed the separation of religion and politics—Church and State, if you will—he wrote in his book *Jesus of Nazareth*, "In his teaching and in his whole ministry, Jesus had inaugurated a non-political Messianic kingdom and had begun to detach these two hitherto inseparable realities from one another." In other words, actually in Jesus' words, we should render to Caesar what is Caesar's, but never should render to Caesar what is God's. These two realities are separated, yet not isolated from each other, but rather intricately connected within the lives of each one of us. On the one hand, the Church benefits from the State to keep and enforce justice. On the other hand, the State benefits from religious beliefs, which help people respond to each other in a moral and respectful way for the good of the "common good." Because of this relationship, Church and State are not each other's opposite, but instead complement each other and support each other.

This principle was further reinforced by the early Church Fathers, as a reaction against the wish of Emperor Constantine and his successors to merge State and Church again in an attempt to control the Church. Let us keep in mind that this line of separation was drawn by the Church, not by the State. After the Protestant Reformation, some states tried again to impose new regulations on churches, while the control of religion was handed over once more to the ruler of each individual State. The religious conflicts were mitigated in 1555 as part of the Peace of Augsburg by the principle that the religion of the ruler, either Catholic or Protestant, is that of the people (*cuius regio, eius religio*). In light of what we discussed earlier, this move was basically un-Christian.

In reaction to situations in which the religion of individuals was made dependent upon the society into which they were born, the United States decided to again separate the Church from the State and give every person the right to choose whatever religion—or lack thereof—one wishes, without any control of the State. The reason behind this separation of Church and State is the free exercise of religion—a principle that originally aimed not at protecting the State from Religion but at protecting Religion from the State. This way, the USA got the First Amendment and its definition of the first freedom: "Congress shall make no law respecting an establishment of religion, or prohibiting the free exercise thereof." Let us call this *secularity*, or "freedom *of* religion."

However, times have changed. Secularism has gone much further in the minds of most secularists. It has gone from "freedom *of* religion" to "freedom *from* religion." Whereas secularity merely separates the non-religious realm from the religious realm, secularism is intolerant of religion and imposes its own totally secular standards and values on everything else, including religion. The only commandment in the life of secularists seems to be, "You shall never invoke the name of God, unless you do so in vain."

So, what is wrong with secularism? There are several

things. Let's start with this one. The claim of secularists—from now on understood as promoting "freedom *from* religion—is in fact inconsistent. These secularists reject any (religious) beliefs, but seem to forget that their own form of secularism is also a (semi-religious) belief in itself—it's a doctrine, a conviction, albeit of a questionable status. Promoting secularism is in essence no different than promoting a religion. One could even make the case that secularism is not just a belief, but as much as a religious belief, so long as we define "religion" vaguely enough. Loosely defined, "religion" is a belief system that moves its members to support a cause with fervent devotion, usually based on the idea that there is some sort of higher power. Well, secularism is not the absence of a belief system, rather it is the very belief that there is no God and that competing belief systems should be rejected or ignored based on the "higher" authority of secularism. To a dedicated secularist the highest power is humanity or society or the state, each one with its secular beliefs and values.

As a matter of fact, everyone has certain "beliefs" and some sort of "faith." So the "secular" cannot possibly be a realm that is free from beliefs or from faith. Yet, that is how many understand the term "secular" nowadays, when they speak of "secular schools," "secular government," "secular values," etc. These terms are now generally understood to mean "free from any beliefs, in particular free from religious beliefs." But it is clear they cannot be free from any beliefs, as the doctrine of secularism—but also other doctrines such as materialism—is at least one of the beliefs still reigning in secularist societies (see Chapter 11). No wonder a State without Religion becomes easily an authoritarian society. As the legendary Archbishop Fulton Sheen put it, "Once a nation ceases to believe, it begins to obey [the Omnipotent State]." Then he quotes William Penn, the founder of

Pennsylvania, who warned us: "Men must be governed by God or they will be ruled by tyrants."

Besides, secularism is not a harmless, neutral doctrine. It creates its own set of beliefs. It believes that Religion is a threat to the State, the Society, and the Culture. It rejects the impact, not so much of any beliefs—for secularism itself is a belief—but in particular of specific *religious* beliefs. We see Western secularization crossing the line here from neutrality to outright hostility toward religion in general, and Catholicism in particular. As Bishop Barron says about secularism, "Accordingly, it wants Catholicism off the public stage and relegated to a private realm where it cannot interfere with secularism's totalitarian agenda."

Another problem of secularism is that it considers all religious beliefs, other than its own beliefs, of the same poor quality—mere opinions. It does not acknowledge that some religious beliefs have a strong basis in rationality and can be defended with rational arguments. Only religious beliefs that are not against reason and can be defended by reason and convey truth are of the right quality (see Chapter 2). As the emeritus Amherst College professor Hadley Arkes points out, non-Catholics must be able to grasp *through reason alone* why they are obliged to respect certain religious beliefs— even though they themselves are non-Catholics and do not understand and respect the religion of those whose beliefs they are commanded to respect. Even in a secular state, we can use our power of reasoning to find out what is true or false when it comes to beliefs, even religious beliefs. There is no valid reason to reject all religious beliefs.

Then there is a third problem with secularism. A secular society is not free of values but creates its own "values." It introduces its own values— the greatest of all values being inclusivity—while excluding religion and rejecting any values that come from religion. In many countries, society used to be "ruled" by religious doctrines of the Church, but nowadays it is controlled by secular doctrines of media and academia. This is possible because the term "value" is actually ill-defined. It covers the entire range from material values to spiritual values to moral values. This ambiguity mixes them up and thus makes us lose sight of the huge differences between them. Since secularists consider all our achievements man-made, they also believe that we can make our own values and rules; so all our values are believed to be man-made as well.

As a consequence, our secularized age has become crammed with new "values." Corporations and universities, for example, are proud to tout their "values." Politicians in secularist societies often say, for instance, that certain policies go against their "values," but what they actually mean is that these policies go against their political wishes. What secularists call their "values" are typically "values" based on support for abortion, euthanasia, homosexuality, and the like. They are values that are as fleeting as the ever-changing value of houses and stock. In this context, it makes sense for Peter Kreeft to exclaim, "God did not give Moses 'The Ten Values.'" The values secularists talk about are no longer associated with ideals and beliefs that are constant, absolute, and objective—which makes for another case of relativism (see Chapter 1).

A fourth problem of secularism is its totalitarian worldview pretention. It pretends to be inclusive but, at the same time, eliminates what it doesn't want to include. As a result, secularism is a totalitarian doctrine that does not accept any light or guidance from anywhere else. It actually makes for a mild form of fascism. Secularists preach tolerance magnanimously, but only for those who agree with them—"my way or no way." This makes Iain T. Benson, a Scottish legal philosopher, question the secularists' agenda as follows: "Are we only to allow all kinds of influence as long as they do not come from religion? Why, for example, ought the beliefs of a politician that originate in materialism be acceptable but a critique of materialism animated by religious convictions be unacceptable?"

Perhaps secularism's main driving force is its anti-religious bias. The secularist society does not allow any mention of God in the public square. It denies there is any religious dimension to a human being, so it has a severely impoverished picture of human beings (see Chapter 5). It does not acknowledge that religion has something to contribute to society that the State cannot provide on its own. Religion is actually needed to fill the voids the State leaves behind, to challenge the State when human dignity is in danger, to heal the wounds the State may cause, to answer questions the State is not familiar with. What this omission in a secularist society leads to is the disappearance of God— or what the Jewish philosopher Martin Buber called "the eclipse of God."

When speaking about religious freedom in Philadelphia, Pope Francis stressed how our various religious traditions "remind us of the transcendent dimension of human existence and our irreducible freedom in the face of every claim to absolute power." Then he added, "We need but look at history, especially the history of the last century, to see the atrocities perpetrated by systems which claimed to build one or another 'earthly paradise' by dominating peoples, subjecting them to apparently indisputable principles and denying them any kind of rights." It couldn't be put more clearly.

A fifth problem of secularism is its assumption that all values and motives derived from religion, especially Christianity, are worthless for the state and for society. In contrast, it should be argued that the Catholic Church has indeed much to offer to society. She does not exist for herself but for the transformation of the world—for the sake of the unborn, the rejected, the disabled, the elderly, the poorest of the poor. It is part of the Church's identity to contribute to society and the common good. The Catholic religion wants to make society a better place to live in—for the *entire* person, not just for a person's material needs. There are many dimensions to a human being—biological, emotional, social, moral, and last but not least religious. Leaving any of these out would be an injustice to any human being.

Ironically, secularists accuse the Catholic Church of exclusiveness—which is considered the worst offense against their secular value of inclusiveness. Doesn't the Church exclude thieves, fornicators, adulterers, wife-beaters, homosexuals, members of the Mafia, etc.? No, she doesn't. Being bad doesn't get you kicked out of the Catholic Church. In fact, the Church claims that she exists for the sake of bad people—she exists for the purpose of helping bad people become good.

As a matter of fact, the Church has much to offer to society that the State cannot. Interestingly enough, secularist parents want to give their children the best they know of in health care and education, but when it comes to religion, they give them nothing, letting them make their own choice of religion at the time they are grown up. Why not do the same then with education? Well, that's one of the many inconsistencies of secularism.

Tom Peterson (MyGodsBlog.com) has beautifully summarized what we, as the Catholic Church, have done for society: We started hospitals to care for the sick; we establish orphanages, and help the poor; we are the largest charitable organization on the planet, bringing relief and comfort to those in need; we educate more children than any other scholarly or religious institution; we founded the college system; we defend the dignity of all human life, and uphold marriage and family; we are...... the Catholic Church... with over one billion in our family sharing in the sacraments and fullness of Christian faith.

Some side effects of Secularism

Secularism has infiltrated the mindset of many people nowadays. It has also affected various institutions by changing them from "religious" to "secular." The most affected institution is probably education. What did secularism do to education?

Many great North American universities were once clearly and openly religious and began under religious auspices and for religious purposes—Harvard, Yale, Princeton, the University of Chicago, Boston University, to name just some of the most prominent. They have become purely secular, or even secularist—indistinguishable from their non-religious counterparts, except for spacious and now largely unused chapels. Catholic colleges and universities have mostly followed the same course. These institutions, which should be educating Catholics to critically examine the conditions of the culture they live in, have instead become the main vehicle by which Catholics are indoctrinated into the secularist "values" of their surroundings. Apparently, conformity with the surrounding culture of secularism ranks higher at these institutions than supporting a culture steeped in religious beliefs and moral values. In universities today, students can find more classes in Buddhism, Islam, or African tribal culture than they can find courses on Plato, Cicero, or Dante—let alone Aristotle, Aquinas, and Augustine.

How should the Catholic Church respond to this development? The best way is probably what she persistently used to do in the past—to be leaven in the world, light that shines in the darkness, or salt that preserves society. Catholic education in the USA, for example, came about when the Church realized public education did not give her new generation as much as necessary for a human being to become a "complete being," which necessarily includes a religious dimension. The Church's response was not a retreat into seclusion, challenged by public education, but rather an engagement to prepare Catholics better for their service to society based on their Catholic faith.

We need something similar today. To preserve their Catholic identity in a secularist world, Catholics should cultivate their identity, not by building walls but by breaking them down, not by constructing road-blocks but by building bridges—in other words, by engaging in society to serve her better through what Catholicism has to offer society. Once you lose your identity and don't know who you are, the wind can turn you in any direction.

Given all of the above, we must come to the conclusion that secularism is a doctrine which is not only seriously flawed but also very destructive.

5. Humanism

What is Humanism?

There are many, many kinds of humanism. St. Augustine was a humanist, St. Thomas More was a humanist—to name just a few religious giants. The only thing most kinds of humanism have in common is that they honor a special place for Man. Humanism in its most general form is a doctrine that emphasizes the value and role of Man in society. The problems come in when we try to define who Man is.

No wonder, then, that humanism has come in many varieties, but today humanism typically refers to a non-religious form of humanism, usually called *secular humanism*, centered on human autonomy and looking to science rather than religion to understand who Man is. In the rest of this chapter, we will focus only on this kind of humanism.

Since secular humanism is not a unified organization and is in a state of constant flux, it is hard to pinpoint what it really stands for. The main outlines, though, can be found in the *Humanist Manifesto* which is the title of three manifestos laying out a Humanist worldview. These three manifestos are the original Humanist Manifesto (1933, often referred to as Humanist Manifesto I), the Humanist Manifesto II (1973), and Humanism and Its Aspirations (2003, a.k.a. Humanist Manifesto III).

Manifesto I was issued with thirty-four signees, among

whom was the famous educator John Dewey. The Manifesto talked of a new "religion", and referred to Humanism as a religious movement to transcend and replace previous religions that were based on allegations of supernatural revelation. It utterly trumpeted the idea that religion is steeped in doctrines which, according to the humanists, "have lost their significance and which are powerless to solve the problem of living in the Twentieth Century." This explains why it also stated that "humanists regard the universe as self-existing and not created."

Manifesto II was even much more explicit about its atheistic foundation, so traditional religion took more of a beating. Among the oft-quoted lines from this 1973 Manifesto are, "No deity will save us; we must save ourselves," and "We are responsible for what we are and for what we will be." One of its principles says very explicitly in its second tenet: "Promises of immortal salvation or fear of eternal damnation are both illusory and harmful."

Manifesto III is deliberately much shorter and less antagonistic to traditional religion, but it still has an anti-religious undertone—for example, in its principle that "Knowledge of the world is derived by observation, experimentation, and rational analysis." Then it says, "Humanists recognize nature as self-existing."

There have been other "manifestos" ever since, but they mainly differ in focus and specifics. The tenets and principles of humanism evidently are presumed to evolve with the culture in time. There are at least two humanist associations who follow this evolution and keep promoting secular humanism. Here are two of them.

The *American Humanist Association* (AHA) summarizes its stand as follows: "Humanism is a progressive life stance that, without theism or other supernatural beliefs, affirms our ability and responsibility to lead meaningful, ethical lives capable of adding to the greater good of humanity."

The *British Humanist Association* (BHA) describes itself as, "working on behalf of non-religious people who seek to live ethical and fulfilling lives on the basis of reason and humanity. It promotes a secular state." It also explicitly states, "Positive atheists—humanists—simply believe that within the confines of a mortal life and the Universe we live in, we have all the resources we need to live meaningful and ethical lives."

So in general it could be said that secular humanism is based on what the philosopher Charles Taylor calls the "sovereign self." It is a philosophy of life which views man as the "supreme being" on Earth, so there is no need for or no space left for a Supreme Being in Heaven. This kind of humanism declares human beings as fully sufficient in themselves, fully self-made, and in complete control of their own history. Humanism declares humanity as the measure of all things.

What is wrong with Humanism?

There is nothing wrong with humanism in its general form, but probably the most striking part of secular humanism is that it has religious roots which it gradually tried to sever. Its roots go way back to St. Augustine, who is widely seen as the father of humanism. After all, part of the core of Augustine's philosophy—which concerned the self, rational introspection, and the importance of reason to our ability to understand ourselves and our nature—was the human search for understanding ourselves, which goes ultimately back to the Biblical idea that we were created in the image of God. True self-knowledge, then, is also a matter of coming into communion with the Divine.

Ironically, at a time when humanists want the power to

self-identify, they rob this ability from God. God is Absolute Being, which means he relies or depends on nothing in order to be himself. He is perfect and, therefore, completely knows Himself. In contrast, all human beings are "contingent" beings, which means they are unable to bring or keep themselves in existence. They don't have sufficient knowledge to self-identify since they do not possess a complete grasp of themselves. They are a mystery even to themselves. So to grow in an authentic knowledge of themselves, they must seek enlightenment from God. That's where they discover their human dignity.

So ultimately, humanism cannot exist without the Judeo-Christian concept of human dignity. Christianity emphasizes the dignity of each individual: Man was created in the image and likeness of God. That's where Man's self-understanding comes from. It is through this Judeo-Christian insight that St. Augustine could develop his anthropology. It was Augustine's anthropology that helped shape and form the emergence of humanism during the ages to come. During the Renaissance, with its "self-affirmation of the free personality," humanism could flourish in a Christian environment. In other words, this incipient phase of humanism was not hostile to Christianity at all—actually extremely receptive.

Those Judeo-Christian roots are hard, if not impossible, to deny. Yet, new developments of humanism, beginning with the Enlightenment, would gradually sever the spiritual and cultural continuity between itself and the Christian religion. In our own day, secular humanism has burned virtually every bridge leading back to its religious sources— which could easily been seen as a form of suicide or self-destruction.

There is another element of secular humanism that needs a critical assessment—its exclusive focus on Man alone. However, the Man of secular humanism is a "truncated"

Man, who has completely lost his religious dimension. When God disappears from our radar, we also lose an important dimension of our lives. This makes for a vision of the human person that is incomplete, for there is no longer a religious dimension to it. It paints a picture of the world in which there is no place for God. It is a picture darkened by an eclipse of God.

Once God has been removed from human life, we have not much more left than mere humanism—a "humanism without God." It considers man as the "measure of all things," in spite of the religious belief that Man can only know himself in reference to God. The better we know God, the better we know our deepest self, for we were made in God's image. As Pope John Paul II put it, "Without the Creator, the creature disappears." When we throw God out, we throw Man out too—and therefore, paradoxically, secular humanism as well. If Man legitimizes himself to be Man, then by the same principle he is the highest authority and can legitimize himself to be not-man, or even in-human.

Another problem of secular humanism is its ambiguous stand regarding religion. On the one hand, it portrays itself sometimes as a religion. On the other hand, it wants to eradicate all forms of religion. This conflict can be well seen in the United States Supreme Court case *Torcaso v. Watkins*. It has been argued that in this case, the Supreme Court agreed that secular humanism is a religion. In the 1961 decision, Justice Hugo Black commented in a footnote, "Among religions in this country which do not teach what would generally be considered a belief in the existence of God are Buddhism, Taoism, Ethical Culture, Secular Humanism, and others." Notice the inclusion of Secular Humanism. Clearly, the Court understood religion to include non-theistic religions such as Secular Humanism.

Yet, the Supreme Court refused to rule that the training

which most children receive in public schools in secular humanism is actually religious instruction. Apparently, the Supreme Court has not been consistent in applying its definition of religion to its present interpretation of the First Amendment. If the no-establishment clause of the First Amendment really means that there should be a wall of separation between religion and the state, why are only theistic religions being forced out of the public square, specifically Christianity? So if Secular Humanism is considered a religion, why then is it allowed to be taught in public schools? Under the guise of separation of Church and State, the courts are actually encouraging, and in fact, funding the teaching of secular humanism, while discriminating against traditional religions.

This ambiguity was as much as acknowledged by Leo Pfeffer, the Humanist attorney who defended the Torcaso case. He realized the status of being a religion could have a "boomerang effect." He feared that if the Supreme Court would uphold its current understanding of religion to include Secular Humanism and therefore would have to order the teachings of Humanism to be removed from the public schools, "the consequences may be no less than the disintegration of our public school system." Doesn't it look like secular humanism is a "public" religion, whereas traditional religions are considered "private"? Yes, it does—unless one uses two different standards. There is no other explanation, unless we accept an inconsistence within secular humanism: it intends itself to be a religion, and, at the same time, it intends to deny this title to any other traditional or competing set of beliefs. Although masked under the guise of being "open" to others, tolerant concerning other "lifestyles," and non-judgmental of others' beliefs, the secular humanists are actually extremely closed, intolerant of, and judgmental concerning any traditional religious belief whatsoever.

Another element of secular humanism that needs a critical analysis is its self-centeredness. At the core of secular humanism is the tendency to view human existence as self-sufficient and self-enclosed. The document *Gaudium et Spes* (59 GS 20 § 2) from Vatican II says that those who profess atheistic humanism, "maintain that it gives man freedom to be an end unto himself, the sole artisan and creator of his own history." In this view, Man has finally become aware that Man alone is responsible for the fulfillment of his dreams, and that Man himself has the power to achieve those. This means that Man is seen as responsible for his own secular salvation.

Obviously, humanism is Self-centered (auto-nomous), whereas Christianity is fundamentally God-centered (theo-nomous). Christianity with its goal of the salvation of Man, relies ultimately upon grace, whereas humanism with its goal of human maturity relies ultimately upon the intuition and ethical will of self-sufficient and independent human beings. The "heathens" of the humanist type just have no need to believe in God because they think they are completely self-sufficient. They do not need God, they do not even want God, because such a God would undermine the foundation of secular humanism—the power of Man, the power of "Me, myself, and I."

The Catechism (2126) considers this "a false conception of human autonomy, exaggerated to the point of refusing any dependence on God." Autonomy does not mean that we can become whatever we please, without being accountable to anyone. Autonomy means instead that we become more and more aware of our deepest self. We understand ourselves best in the light of God. But secular humanism rejects that dimension.

Then there is another inconsistency in secular humanism. It rejects the notion of God, yet it keeps the idea hiding behind it. It makes Man a god in himself and gives Man a divine nature that only belongs to God. It assigns the status of a Primary Cause to a mere secondary cause, Man (see Chapter 3). However, if Man has any power, it's God's power—a received power. If Man has any power, it's power received from God, not from "self." So by rejecting God, humanists actually remove the source of Man's power, and thus undermine Man's power itself. As the Apostle Paul said, "[They] worshipped and served the creature more than the Creator." (Rom. 1:25). Since the existence of our world is contingent, not a necessity and not self-explanatory, our world would be nothing, literally, if there were no Creator God.

As a matter of fact, Man is not god. The Judeo-Christian tradition makes that very clear. However, this is entirely contrary to secular humanism, which appeals to the oldest vice in the world—the human desire to be "like gods." Satan put it so cleverly, "your eyes will be opened and you will be like gods" (Gen. 3:5). If we embrace this kind of humanism, we are promised total freedom to make our own decisions, to form our own moral code, to violate rules concerning social and moral behavior without any restraint. It enshrines selfishness and self-centeredness, and turns them into a virtue.

Indeed, for many people, belief in God has been replaced by belief in god-like humans. Humanism has no longer any need of God. The Man of humanism is setting out on his own to know and master his cosmos—all of it. The Catechism (2124) explains how secular humanism "falsely considers man to be 'an end to himself, and the sole maker, with supreme control, of his own history.'"

Another questionable element of secular materialism is its highly optimistic outlook on Man's power. The Humanist Manifesto gave humanism the ability to solve the woes of the twentieth century, but by doing so, it inadvertently signed its own death warrant. After the horrific experiences of the two world wars of the 20th century, it should no longer be possible to formulate phrases like "the destiny of man" or the "triumph of human reason" without an instant consciousness of the folly and brutality they drag behind them. It is actually almost impossible to think of a crime that has not been committed in the name of Man's power.

This also shows us there is no room in secular humanism for any limitations on Man's power. It pretends that all our problems—personal, social, technological, and what have you—can be entirely solved by using the right human knowledge, technology, reasoning, and judgment. We are supposed to be in full control of ourselves and should further free ourselves through economic, scientific, technological, and social liberation. However, even science hasn't been able to solve all our problems. This is an especially bitter outcome, because the humane project of the modern sciences was the great hope and, in many respects, the great success, of humanism. Today, it is actually regarded by most humanists as a curse. In any case, modern science has made secular humanism itself an outdated doctrine.

The same holds for any human problems, such as suffering, that humanism cannot solve on its own. The Humanist Manifesto actually tries to deprive Man of some of the very obstacles that propel him to greater deeds and that help him refine his character. We should ask humanists what to do when disaster strikes us, when things do not go the way we had planned, when we become victims of injustice in our man-made systems—in short, when self-made people reach their own limits? Don't we all know that life doesn't owe us a living? Suffering actually shows us that we are not in control of our lives but need divine assistance. In addition, we should ask these humanists: isn't it striking that Christianity actually has the Cross at center stage in its religion; it claims there is some mysterious salvation for us in carrying our personal crosses in life—for the benefit of ourselves and the benefit of others. No wonder the Cross is a touchstone for Christians, but at the same time a stumbling block for non-Christians, including many humanists. For Christians, salvation comes through Jesus' Cross—for humanists, it comes only through human efforts.

Perhaps the most serious flaw of Humanism is its image of Man as "good by nature." This misconception goes back to Jean-Jacques Rousseau (1712-1778) who believed that Man is naturally good and that vice and error are alien to him. In his own words, "If man is left... to his own notions and conduct, he would certainly turn out the most preposterous of human beings." (True, Rousseau does acknowledge that children must be guided in order to facilitate their natural, good tendencies.) In a sense, there is some truth to this. Genesis 1 says that God indeed declared humanity "good," having created Man in the image of God. We can see the goodness of humanity all around us, but the other part of the truth is that there is also something definitely wrong with humanity. The main message of Genesis 3 is that humanity has chosen to determine what is good all by itself, without any reference to God, which is called the "Fall." That's why the Church says that human nature is good but corrupted. You don't have to be a scholar of history to see what the Fall has led to. Just think of all the horrendous atrocities committed by human beings over the centuries. Chesterton once called the Original Sin "the only part of Christian theology which can really be proved."

Hardly anyone asks the question, "Why do people do good things? The reason nobody asks that question is that, due to Humanism, our society believes that Man is basically good and therefore we expect him to do good, so we never ask "Why?" We are surprised when someone does bad things instead. The general idea is that Man is basically good, but society makes Man do bad things. A big problem with this view is this: If Man is basically good, how did we get a bad society to begin with? In the eyes of Humanism, the first society would have been made by good people, would have been perfect from the start, and would have stayed perfect. But don't we all know better?

If we really are good by nature, what's the point of Christianity? The Bible tells us the answer: sin! Whereas the creation myths of many cultures hold that good and evil are inherent elements of human nature and the world order—it's supposedly the way things were made—the Book of Genesis corrects this error by revealing that evil is not rooted in creation, but in humanity's abusive decision to turn away from God, from one another, and from God's created order through sin. Because of the Fall, the image of God has been corrupted, and Adam's sin has been passed on to the whole human race, which is called "Original Sin." Although the goodness of their original creation remains, humans are now flawed images of God. But not forever. Christianity is a religion of salvation. Salvation from what? From sin. But if we do have no sin, at least no sin deeply rooted in our nature, who would need Christianity? Who would need the suffering and death of Jesus?

David Carlin says about the idea that underlies doctrines such as Humanism:

> It has led almost everywhere to the triumph of the idea of democracy (if not always actual democracy); for if we are good by nature we can be trusted to govern ourselves. It has led to the universal spread of capitalism; for if we are good by nature,

> *our passion for wealth must be good. It has led to the sexual revolution; for if we are good by nature, we can give free rein to our sexual impulses.*

The contrast between Humanism and Christianity is obvious. The way they treat human nature couldn't be more different. What human nature needs, says Humanism, is a better society and environment—straighten out your surroundings, and you'll all be happy and prosperous and good. What human nature needs, says Christianity in contrast, is repentance for your sins—repent your sins, and you'll be happy and prosperous and good when you reach heaven. The former is a false, unrealistic hope from "below," the latter a harder but much more realistic promise from "Above."

Some side effects of Humanism

Can secular humanists be good without God? Of course they can, for most people, religious or not, do condemn murder. One doesn't have to be a Christian to do good and be a good person. Remember, as they say, "Just be well so you can do good." Humanists have even argued that belief in God only distorts moral motivation.

Although there are some humanists who may be dedicated to humanity because of their belief in God who created us, there are also many more secular humanists who have no longer any need of God, as we found out. The *British Humanist Association*, for instance, explicitly states, "Positive atheists—humanists—simply believe that within the confines of a mortal life and the Universe we live in, we have all the resources we need to live meaningful and ethical lives." These humanists believe it is a mistake to think that we need anything more, or that anything more actually exists. Apparently, belief in God is a waste of time in their eyes. So they go as far as claiming, "The religious element, in fact, distorts moral motivation."

But this raises the question from where humanists derive their motivation of being good and doing good for humanity. It is hard to see how it could be anchored in humanism itself. Why should whites care about blacks, or the rich about the poor, or the strong about the weak? There is nothing in another human being that forces me to do good to them. No society or government has the right to demand my absolute obedience. No other human being has the right to demand absolute obedience from me. No one, not even myself, has the right to demand my absolute obedience. The only authority that can obligate me is someone infinitely superior to me; no one else has that much authority. In other words, there is only one reason for us to do good and be good to others—the reason being that God is our Father who created us all as children of the same God, made in his image and likeness.

Therefore, no one, not even secular humanists, can be good and do good without God. True, they *can* choose to be good and do good, but their reason cannot be that they *ought* to do good. Only those who believe in God do really know that they ought to act right in a moral way, and only they know why certain acts are intrinsically wrong. The atheist Friedrich Nietzsche, of all people, clearly understood that if there is no God—"the death of God," as he called it—then that would be the destruction of all morality in life. Nietzsche saw in all clarity how in a world without divine and eternal laws of moral behavior, neither our dignity nor our morality would be able to survive in the long run, for we would no longer know *why* certain things are not permissible.

Nietzsche basically told us, paraphrased, that secular humanists shelter themselves in caves and venerate shadows of the God they once believed in; they are still holding on to something they cannot provide themselves, mere shadows of their religious past. In secular humanism, they are merely shadows of morality. These shadows preserve the essence of morality without the substance.

Of course, you can be moral without being Christian; you can be moral without knowing why you are a moral being and why you ought to be moral. You certainly don't have to be a Christian to act morally or to know right from wrong, but Christianity may offer us the best explanation of why we should act morally and why certain things are intrinsically right or wrong. Only Christianity can explain to us why we *ought* to do good, why we have the moral *duty* to do good. The answer is: because we owe it to God, and therefore to others.

When humanists do the same good things as Christians, perhaps one could say that they actually are still living off of Judeo-Christian capital—without them even knowing it, or acknowledging it. They are now venerating "shadows of the past," in the words of Nietzsche. Sometimes they base their acts on the Golden Rule, presumably free of religion: "Do to others what you want to be done to yourself" (Tobit 4:15; Matthew 7:12; Luke 6:31). Indeed, the Golden Rule can be found in Christian, Jewish, Islamic, Buddhist, and Confucian texts, among others. As St. Paul says about the Gentiles (Rom. 2:15), "[T]he demands of the law are written in their hearts." That's in the hearts of all people. Yet, a worldview without God looks like a jigsaw puzzle with one large and vital piece missing: take away religion and it just doesn't look complete. So believing in God does not distort moral motivation, as many humanists think, but actually bolsters it, explains it, and grounds is.

So, we must come to the conclusion that secular humanism has in fact eaten away the very foundation of morality. The Russian writer and Nobel Laureate Aleksandr Solzhenitsyn summarized this well in his famous 1978 Harvard commencement address, "A World Split Apart":

> *In American democracy at the time of its birth, all individual human rights were granted because man is God's creature. That is, freedom was given to the individual conditionally, in the assumption of his constant religious responsibility. Such was the heritage of the preceding thousand years. Two hundred or even fifty years ago, it would have seemed quite impossible, in America, that an individual could be granted boundless freedom simply for the satisfaction of his instincts or whims.*

Given all of the above, we must come to the conclusion that secular humanism is a doctrine which is not only seriously flawed but also very destructive.

6. Liberalism

What is Liberalism?

Just as there are many sorts of liberals—liberals in politics, liberals in economics, liberals in religion, liberals in morality, you name it—so there are also many forms of liberalism. In what follows, we will limit the doctrine of liberalism to the domain of *morality*. Put in very simple, crude terms, the master principle of morality is that good is to be done and evil to be avoided. So a simple definition of morality is: doing what is right and avoiding what is wrong. Determining what is right—and therefore what ought to be done—and determining what is wrong—and therefore what ought to be avoided—is done in a *moral code*.

One of the basic tenets of moral liberalism is freedom and tolerance—freedom as to what a person can decide to do in moral terms and tolerance as to what other people can choose to do when it comes to morality. Moral liberalism bestows on everyone the complete freedom to compose one's own personal moral code. There are many options to choose from, of course, but the three main options could be summarized as follows.

Option #1—probably the most popular one in moral liberalism—is that we are allowed to do whatever we decide to call good or to avoid whatever we want to call evil. It is one's personal choice that determines what is right or wrong in morality. To put it differently, I myself make my own moral code, if any. No one has the right to tell me what I ought to do or ought to avoid—I am fully autonomous. So nothing and nobody should stop me from doing what I decide is "right" to do. When I have to make moral choices, any choice I make on my own is per definition right in and of itself. If I want to bully or rape someone, for instance, I have the moral right to do so. No one can stop me from using my own, personalized moral code.

There is a school of thought that comes close to this—it's called hedonism. It argues that pleasure—the pleasure of having food, drinks, drugs, sex, money, and what have you—is the only intrinsic good in life that we should strive for. Hedonism makes pleasure the one and only "good" thing in life. Its moral code, if it deserves that label, defines something "good" in terms of something natural, "pleasure." Thus it makes the claim that life "ought" to be as pleasurable, comfortable, and stimulating as I can make it. If I want to go for pleasure, then that's something I have the moral right to do. My moral code tells me so.

A variant of this option is worded a bit more deceivingly: "Never disobey your own conscience." That sounds like a strong moral stand, but it is basically shorthand for "Do whatever you want." Almost all people have something about conscience that they respect, even if their theory is that conscience is nothing. One wonders how the notion of conscience could become so popular. The main reason probably is that the slogan "Follow your conscience" has come to be code for pursuing one's personal preferences and desires—which is basically option #1. Therefore, you can make any act morally right by claiming you followed your conscience. In this option, following your conscience comes close to a moral code with an empty shell.

Option #2—probably for the more serious thinkers

among us—is that whatever ought to be done or avoided is determined not by us but by our surroundings. As a consequence, it is legislation or the majority vote that determines what is right or wrong in morality. To put it differently, people we live with are the makers of our moral code. When we have to make moral choices, our surroundings tell us which choice is right and which choice is morally wrong. In a world where slavery is accepted, for instance, it is not morally wrong to keep slaves. It only becomes morally wrong when a change in the majority vote or a change in legislation tells us so. Had the slaveholders won the American Civil War, so they say, we might see it today as an admirable institution.

A view that comes very close to this option is utilitarianism. In this view, something is considered morally right depending on its effects—that is, if it leads to "the greater happiness of a greater number of people." Something becomes morally right if it gives more happiness to more people around us. Seen this way, society exists above all to provide for the individual's comfortable self-preservation, but in the greatest possible numbers. In other words, a moral code can be judged by measuring quantities and qualities in our direct surroundings. It makes for a pretty practical approach.

Option #3—probably for the more sophisticated minds among us—is that whatever we choose to do comes with our genes, and is the outcome of our evolutionary history. To put it differently, our moral code is a product of genes. When we have to make moral choices, our genes tell us which choice is right. If evolution promoted polygamy in the human species, for instance, then a man would have the moral right to have several women. This would be considered morally right because our genes make us do it.

Option #3 is very common among those who rely

completely on biology and the theory of evolution for their explanations. How could this option ever become an attractive explanation for a moral code in morality? Well, some scientists and philosophers strongly believe that morality is a genetic issue and that evolutionary biology can explain how humanity acquired its morality (see Chapter 14). Their 'magic wand' is the theory of natural selection. Some use the example of incest. There is, so they say, an almost universal human taboo on incest—phrased as a moral law it says "intercourse with very close relatives is wrong and hence forbidden." Well, the advocates of option #3 would point out that inbreeding between close relatives tends to bring out lethal traits and other afflictions that lessen the offspring's reproductive success. Hence they argue that natural selection has been promoting a genetic basis for behavioral and moral avoidance of intercourse with close relatives.

Another example would be the moral laws given in the fifth and sixth commandments of the Decalogue, "You shall not kill" and "You shall not commit adultery." Some have made the case that humans have become monogamous "by nature," since that would give the offspring a better protection, and that is why natural selection must have promoted monogamy—thus giving the sixth commandment a genetic basis. Others have made the claim that killing any members of the same species would undermine the persistence of the species—hence the prohibition of killing was positively selected for by the process of natural selection. They even consider the moral value of paternal care for children to be a product of natural selection, since fathers who do not feel an "instinctive" responsibility towards their underage children would reduce their offspring's reproductive success. What all these cases have in common is that morality is supposedly based on genes promoted by natural selection. So my moral code seems "personalized" because of the genes I inherited.

These are, in brief, at least three options the doctrine of moral liberalism may take on. What all three options have in common, and what is essential to the doctrine of moral liberalism, is the idea that a moral code is something personal and optional, but not something we ought to do on absolute moral grounds.

What is wrong with Liberalism?

Let's unravel the three options which moral liberalism offers, but in a reversed order, beginning with option #3—whatever we consider morally right is determined by our genes.

The first problem of option #3 is that it is self-destructive. If we believe that our moral code is determined by our genes, we may have to face the possibility that our claims are also determined by our genes, which would undermine those very claims. Think of this. If the theory of natural selection is a product of the human mind—according to a hypothesis generated by Charles Darwin's mind—and at the same time, if the human mind, including its moral code, is supposed to be the product of natural selection, then we end up in a self-destructive vicious circle. Put differently, if Darwin's thoughts were the mere product of natural selection, so would be his science and his idea that the moral code is a genetic product, and as a consequence, none of his thoughts could then be trusted. That would be the end of the theory of natural selection itself and thus of option #3.

But there is another problem with option #3. If our moral code is a product of our genes, there is no more need to speak of a moral code. Yet, most people keep doing that. If morality were encoded in the genes, why would we need an articulated moral rule to reinforce what "by nature" we would or would not desire to do anyway? If morality is encoded in the genes, a moral code would be completely redundant. Instead the opposite could be argued: morality has the power to overrule what our genes dictate—passions, emotions, and drives. If we let passion govern reason, rather than let reason govern passion, there is little hope for morality. The verdict as to what is morally right or wrong is not regulated by genes but by a moral code. If moral behavior were genetic, there would be no need for a moral code as well. We would all act right by mere nature, so there would no longer be talk of acting morally right or wrong.

Yet, people keep doing what is morally wrong. Are they acting against their genes? That's hard to believe. In contrast, one could very well argue that moral laws tell us to do what natural selection does *not* promote and what our genes do *not* make us do "by nature." Reality tells us that far too many people are willing to break a moral rule when they can get away with it. It is hard to believe that they are acting against their genes. Morality is about something that is outside the scope of biology, actually beyond the reach of science. Moral laws such as "You shall not kill" or "You shall not commit adultery" could never make it through natural selection, for their offenders—the killers, the promiscuous, and the rapists—would be much more successful in reproduction than their victims or the ones who go by a moral code. Moral laws do not seem to have any survival value and therefore could hardly be the outcome of natural selection.

Perhaps the most basic problem of option #3 is that reducing a moral issue to a genetic issue cannot do full justice to the moral issue. If we reduce morality to something else—something like natural selection—then we lose exactly that specific feature that makes morality what it is, so we are no longer dealing with morality. The problem with this kind of reduction is that it is likely to sacrifice precisely those features of morality that give it a morally distinctive character. So by "reducing" morality to things like natural selection or genetics, we inevitably lose its distinctive moral character. But how could morality ever come from non-morality? When we define moral notions in non-moral terms, we betray their moral aspect. It is hard to see how non-moral causes such as evolution and natural selection could ever produce a moral effect. If they cannot, then that would be the end of option #3.

Let's move on to option #2—the idea that the moral code is something determined by legislation or by a majority vote. What is wrong with that idea? First of all, moral laws cannot be identified with civil or legal laws that are established by a government. There can actually be quite a discrepancy between these two kinds of laws. In ideal situations, civil laws should be a reflection of moral laws, but often they are not. If the law of the land is not a reflection of the moral law, moral laws become a challenge to civil laws. We saw this, for instance, when Martin Luther King challenged racial segregation in his country while campaigning against unjust civil laws. Therefore, he called any unjust legal or civil law "a code that is out of harmony with the moral law." He could only do so by making a clear distinction between legal laws and moral laws.

But not only are moral laws and civil laws often distinct, there is also another big difference that sets the moral domain apart from the civil domain—which is the difference between what we call "moral rights" and what we call "legal entitlements." The latter are enforced by governments and majority votes, but the former are not. Strangely enough, some people think of moral rights as if they were entitlements that the government gives us. True, we gain entitlements as we age—US citizens can drive a car at sixteen, can vote at eighteen, can buy alcohol at twenty-one. Entitlements are enforced by a legal system—the laws of the land.

But we cannot apply this kind of reasoning to human rights. Protection of a human being is not a conditional legal entitlement, but an unconditional moral right. It does not progress with age, but is rooted in the fact that we are dealing with a human being from the very beginning. There is no gradualism when it comes to human rights; killing a thirty-year-old person, for instance, is not worse than killing a twenty-year-old one. The command "Thou shalt not kill" is not merely a form of pacifism but also pertains to killing innocent human lives in the womb. In other words, there is a fundamental difference between the moral right to life and the entitlements we were given to vote or drive.

More in general, each one of us has human rights because they are based on a universal moral code. Entitlements we only have because we belong to a certain society. The government can hand out entitlements, but it cannot give us moral laws and moral rights—neither can it take those away, although it may sometimes try to. Unlike entitlements, moral laws, values, and rights are universal, absolute, timeless, objective, and nonnegotiable standards of human behavior. They come with the fact that we are human beings.

A third problem with option #2 is that we would never be able to evaluate, calibrate, or weigh differences between moral codes, because they would all be worth the same in being enforced by a government or by a majority vote. Yet, most of us would agree that we do not consider all moral codes to be of the same quality. Think, for instance, of the Nuremberg trials that took place after World War II—or of any other international court, for that matter. Seen from a purely legal point of view, it would not have been right, or even possible, to bring to trial and punish the Nazi perpetrators who had applied the civil laws that were created and implemented by a regime that had come to power through legal channels—for they were just "law-abiding" citizens following the law of the land. But seen from a universal moral code perspective, their "lawful" actions were atrocities committed against humanity. Somehow, we seem to have some agreement on a more general and universal understanding of the moral code. This is obviously contrary to what option #2 claims.

A fourth problem with option #2 is that it considers moral laws as volatile and time-dependent as civil or legal laws are. The latter can change when the government changes or when the majority changes its vote. But the former appear to be quite different. True, moral laws are part of a moral code. However, when the moral code changes, that does not mean the moral laws are changing too. This statement probably needs more explanation. Let's try to do so by going back to the notion of "moral values" (see Chapter 4). Moral values are associated with moral laws, but they add something more specific.

In morality, the term "moral value" has a very specific meaning. As C. S. Lewis once put it, "The human mind has no more power of inventing a new value than of imagining a new primary color." The "moral eye" sees values in life, just like the "physical eye" sees colors in nature. That's the reason why moral *values* should not be confused with moral *evaluations*. Moral evaluations are merely our personal feelings or discernments regarding moral values. Secularists think that, in making moral evaluations, we create moral values in accordance with these evaluations. So when evaluations change, the moral values and laws are said to change as well.

If that were true, our moral values would indeed be subject to various cultural, historical, and genetic changes.

But that conclusion is based on a confusion of terms. True, the moral code may appear to change over time, but that does not mean moral laws and moral values are changing as well. Apparently, option #2 pretends to be about moral values, but it is actually dealing with moral evaluations. Moral evaluations are merely a reflection of the way we discern absolute moral values and react to them for the time being. Moral evaluations may change over time, but moral values do not—they are absolute, universal, and timeless.

Then we have option #1 left—one creates one's own personal moral code as one pleases. This is arguably the most popular option of moral liberalism nowadays. In this view, a person's moral code is geared towards reaching a specific outcome—in most cases, more pleasure or more happiness. That outcome is supposed to determine a person's "moral" choices and actions. According to this option, if pleasure or happiness is your "moral" goal, then go for it, for it is supposedly also "good" in a moral sense.

The problem of this option is not so much that the target of more pleasure or happiness is questionable but the mere fact that morality is reduced to reaching something else, a certain goal or target. The problem of this view is that it treats moral laws as if they were *instrumental* laws—that is, relative laws which tell us what we need to do in order to attain something else. Once we consider morally right anything that leads to more pleasure or more happiness, we are making those acts instrumental to a certain goal or purpose. True, something can be called "good" in relation to a given goal or purpose. Medical rules and procedures, for instance, are "good" for the purpose of medical care. Such rules are always instrumental because they tell us what we need to do in order to attain something else. They are of the form "If you want X, do Y." If anyone ever wonders why a certain act (Y) is "good" in this instrumental sense, we can provide an explanation in terms of its objective (X). If the act does meet its objective, it is considered "good," and if it does not meet the objective, it is consequently "wrong." But this doesn't mean that those actions are also right or wrong in a moral sense.

In contrast to instrumental rules, moral laws, rules, and values are absolute, because they tell us what we ought to do as human beings, irrespective of any other objective; hence they are often called *intrinsic*. They are ends-in-themselves— and not, like instrumental laws or rules, means-to-other- ends. In other words, there's nothing "useful" about moral laws and values. If anyone ever wonders why a certain act is good in a moral sense, we have no explanation to offer and cannot refer to other ends; all we can say is, "It's evidently right to act this way, and wrong to not act this way." It is a matter of self-evidence. The moral value of human life, for instance, is self-evident, whereas the technique of certain medical treatments is only right if and as long as it works to reach its objective.

But there is more. Not only are moral laws and values self-evident, they are also *universal*—that is, they don't fit in a personalized moral code. Morality does not come with a specific race, ethnicity, nation, party, or church—it is a common property that belongs to *all* human beings. Morality is not connected with interest groups or with majority votes, but it is universal in scope—it demands the same of everyone everywhere. Because of this, moral laws and values are universally applicable to all of humanity, regardless of race, ethnicity, nationality, culture, or political affiliation.

Those who deny the universality of moral laws are basically relativists who privatize and politicize moral laws as if they were merely part of a personal moral code. This makes Peter Kreeft exclaim, "In fact, the moral language that everyone uses every day—language that praises, blames, counsels, or commands—would be strictly meaningless if relativism were true." Morality is about universal laws and values in this world; these tell us what we ought to do—no matter what, whether we like it or not, whether we feel it or not.

Let's wrap up this discussion. After all of the above, we must come to the conclusion that the three options moral liberalism has come up with are all unable to explain where our moral code comes from. Besides, they cannot account for the fact that the moral code and its moral laws and moral values have some puzzling characteristics: They are intrinsic, universal, absolute, and timeless. Morality tells us that we do not have the right to make our own personal moral code. What we ought to do or ought to avoid is not up to our genes, our surroundings, or our personal choices. We do not have the right to replace moral values—which are absolute, universal, and time-less—with our own moral evaluations—which are relative, individual, and fleeting.

Some side effects of Liberalism

Moral liberalism denies that there is an *objective* moral world of rights and wrongs, independent of us. However, once we start to question the idea that there is an objective moral world of rights and wrongs, then the idea of an objective cognitive world of truths and untruths will also hang in the balance. I would like to make the case here that there is a close resemblance between these two worlds. Moral laws are somewhat comparable to the laws of nature science deals with. I think the upcoming comparison between moral laws and scientific laws may be quite enlightening.

There are some interesting parallels between the laws of science and the laws of morality. First of all, both of them are universal (applicable to everyone everywhere). The scientific law of gravity, for instance, holds for the entire universe. And the moral law that forbids murder, for example, applies to everyone everywhere. Second, both of them are considered *objective*—being a "given" that's independent of us and of any human authority. In other words, scientific laws and moral laws are not invented but need to be discovered. Therefore, they are something "real"—not just mental creations that pop up in our minds. Third, both of them are timeless—even if we do not know the underlying law yet. Just as "scientific laws are true," even when we do not know yet they are true, "moral laws are right," even though we may not realize yet they are morally right. This means they are true or right, regardless of whether or not we know them to be true or right.

The last point may need some further explanation. Let's start with science. Our current understanding of scientific laws is a work in progress and constantly needs revision each time we reach a better understanding of those laws in the way they really are. In the meantime, we assume there are absolute and universal laws of nature, although we may not yet have fully captured them in our current understanding and in our existing evaluations. The law of gravity, for instance, was already true before Isaac Newton discovered that law, but we didn't know it yet.

Something similar holds for moral laws and values. Slavery is a case in point. A few centuries ago, slavery was not evaluated as morally wrong, but nowadays it is by most people. As we said before, our moral evaluations may have changed, but that does not mean moral laws and values did too. Only some people in the past—moral giants such as St. Cyprian, St. Gregory of Nyssa, St. John Chrysostom, St. Patrick, St. Anselm, St. Vincent de Paul, to name just a few— were able to discern the timeless moral law that prohibits slavery. However, many of their contemporaries were blind for this moral law. Anyone who does not see the evidence of moral laws is morally blind. Although a blind person cannot see the trees outside, the trees are still there; the existence of the trees does not depend on whether the blind person perceives them or not. In a similar way a morally blind person cannot see the moral laws and values out there, yet they are there; their existence does not depend on whether a person with moral blindness does perceive them or not.

Often we may need "visionaries" who do see clearly what is morally right. We need such people to show us the disconnect that may exist between what we think is right and what is in fact right. It is not always right to obey our culture's values. Just as science needs geniuses like Newton and Einstein to discover scientific laws which no one else had seen before them, so morality also needs "geniuses" such as Moses, Prophets, and Saints to uncover moral laws that others were blind for. We certainly can see farther and better by standing on the shoulders of giants. Just like we should not lower standards in school teaching when some cannot make the mark, we should not adjust moral standards to what everyone can handle or is willing to handle.

No matter how moral laws are discovered, whether sooner or later, we still need to raise the question of where these objective, universal, absolute, and timeless moral laws come from. Since we argued in this chapter against moral liberalism which claims that moral laws and values come from our genes, our surroundings, or our own desires, we must come up with a better answer as to where they really come from. That answer is, in a nutshell, that they do not come from "below" but from "above." What does that mean?

Moral laws were engraved into nature by the Creator; they are part of the way this world was created and designed by the Creator. There is a moral order in nature as much as there is a physical order in nature. Just as our physiological nature makes it necessary for us to eat certain foods and to breathe oxygen for our bodies to be healthy, so our moral nature makes certain moral rules and values necessary for our souls to be healthy. In other words, moral laws come from Heaven! You don't have to be a Christian to know this. Even an atheist such as the French philosopher Jean-Paul Sartre realized that there can be no absolute and objective standards of right and wrong, if there is no eternal Heaven that would make moral laws and values objective and universal. Moral values and laws reside in Heaven. This was also acknowledged by the drafters of the *United States Declaration of Independence* when they declared that we are endowed by our Creator with certain unalienable Rights—not man-made but God-given. Only God can demand absolute obedience from us—no one and nothing else can.

Once we lose sight of God and lead a life "as if there is no God," we may also lose the foundation of morality, because we no longer know *why* certain things are not permissible. Without moral laws and values from Heaven, we could even lose our judicial laws, which have been protecting us so far to the extent they were rooted in moral laws. All of this may ultimately lead to the nihilism of no-law, no-authority, no-morality, and no-purpose in life. When Aleksandr Solzhenitsyn, in his 1983 Templeton Prize lecture, tried to locate the root of the evils of the 20th century—two world wars, three totalitarian regimes with death camps, and a Cold War—he discerned a profound truth: "Men have forgotten God." What does this lead to? In his novel *The Brothers Karamazov*, Fyodor Dostoyevsky had already asked Man: "how is he going to be good without God?" That's the million-dollar question! Dostoyevsky answered that question himself when he warned us that without God, all things are permissible.

Given all of the above, we must come to the conclusion that moral liberalism is a doctrine which is not only seriously flawed but also very destructive.

7. Genderism

What is Genderism?

Before we discuss what the doctrine of genderism asserts, let's find out first what "gender" stands for. The term "gender" was introduced in 1955 to distinguish it from the term "sex." Someone's sex is biologically determined. It determines whether we are born as a boy or a girl. A baby's sex is basically established at the time of conception. The egg cell always carries one X chromosome, but the sperm cell can introduce either an X or a Y chromosome into the egg cell. If the egg cell is fertilized by a Y-bearing sperm cell, the new organism is a boy (XY), but if it is fertilized is by an X-bearing sperm cell, the new baby is a girl (XX).

After fertilization, development is "steered" in one of two directions, male or female. At the 10th week, the penis of the male is slightly larger than the clitoris of the female. At the 12th week, the male scrotum has formed from the tissue that becomes the labia major in the female. Finally, at the 34th week, the distinctive features of the genitalia of the two sexes are fully present. Therefore, at birth, the anatomical differences between male and female are practically unmistakable. When the baby is born, the obstetrician or midwife announces, "It's a boy" (M) or "It's a girl" (F)—and it will stay that way.

But once the newborn has been "declared" a boy or a girl

on a birth certificate, based on anatomical and sexual characteristics, new features develop that make them either more masculine or more feminine. During the further development, the difference between boys and girls becomes much more than a difference in biological characteristics—namely, differences in behavioral traits, social roles, and cultural expectations that come with being a man or a woman in a given society. As soon as parents know the sex of their child, they treat the child either as a boy or a girl. Early on in human development, parents as well as society take on a "molding" role.

This particular aspect of development is usually captured with the term *gender*. Whereas sex is engrained in our chromosomes, gender is acquired, partly based on cultural restrictions, partly on personal choices. To put it simply, sex is what you are biologically; gender is what you become socially. In other words, the terms "male" and "female" are sex categories, while the labels "masculine" and "feminine" are gender categories. The distinction between sex and gender is generally accepted nowadays and seems to be fair game. According to the *World Health Organization*, sex refers to the biological and physiological characteristics that define men and women, whereas gender refers to the socially constructed roles, behaviors, activities, and attributes that a given society considers appropriate for men and women.

So far so good. But here is where the doctrine or ideology of genderism kicks in. Genderism has redefined "gender." It is no longer understood as a social construct, but as referring to the sex a person identifies with. Therefore, some people may feel that their soul is "trapped" in the body of the opposite sex. If a male identifies with the female sex, so genderism claims, then that must be his, or now her, "real" sex—and therefore, doctors must make it come true. In this view, sex is no longer a biological concept, but it has become a social construct too.

Genderism insists that we are not born as "F" or "M" but as "X," so that we can then later decide whether we want to be "F," "M," or anything in between. Your sex is no longer something you were born with, but merely something arbitrarily declared on your birth certificate. If John says he is a women, then John is a woman—that is a matter of fact and fairness. The gender dogma states it very clearly: We are who we say we are, if we say so.

Consequently, if some people feel that their soul is "trapped" in the body of the opposite sex, then the opposite sex must be their "real" sex, so doctors must *make* that come true. Not surprisingly, in the medical field, a new syndrome was constructed, called "gender identity disorder." Because the term "disorder" was considered controversial in circles of genderism believers, the new label became "gender dysphoria." This called for a new diagnosis and a series of proper treatments, including trans-gender surgery and hormone replacement therapy. Now we end up with men and women as well as transgender men and transgender women.

Another development is that genderism has even invaded places such as restrooms, locker-rooms, and shower facilities of schools and other institutions in several countries. In the name of anti-discrimination policies, transgender individuals must be allowed access to the facilities consistent with their "gender identity." What previous generations took for granted—namely, that words such as *man, woman, mother,* and *father* name natural realities combined with social roles—is now increasingly regarded as obsolete.

What is wrong with Genderism?

Genderism may appear as a rather recent discovery—and in a way it is—but it has much older philosophical roots.

There are at least two philosophical traditions that have fed into it: the dualism of Gnostic assumptions as well as the dualism of Cartesian assumptions. We discussed already what Gnosticism preaches (see Chapter 3). All Gnostics, ancient and modern, believe that the soul is trapped in the body and needs to be freed from this dungeon. The other tradition goes back to René Descartes, who not only tended to separate body and soul, but even set them against each other in an antagonistic relationship—a master/slave relationship, so to speak. Consequently, the body is often seen also as a prison from which the soul wants to escape.

Unfortunately for genderism, the tenets of gnostic and Cartesian dualism are very dubious. Dualism sets the soul in opposition to the body, based on the mistaken belief that only the soul is considered the "real me," thus leaving the body at the mercy of the soul or as a prison for the soul. In this view, an entirely isolated soul can decide on its own what the body should be like—for instance, male or female. What is lost in this approach is the fact that body and soul form a unity, with the soul expressing itself through the body.

The body is always a person's body, and the soul is always a person's soul. Ultimately, we cannot separate the body from the soul nor can we treat the soul as separate from the body—they are both united in one person. Although we can mentally distinguish between our bodies and our souls, that does not make them divisible in practice. The fact that we can distinguish a flame's heat from its light does not mean that we can separate the heat from the light.

Consequently, the body cannot be seen as a prison from which the soul wants to escape. A person is not merely a body or machine manipulated by the soul—a person *is* a body with a soul. Neither is a human being merely a soul. It is not so that the soul is at the mercy of the body, neither is the body ruled by a tyrannical soul. In other words, there is no such thing as a disembodied soul, nor is there a soul-less human body. A body without a soul is a corpse; a soul without a body is what we usually call a ghost. Body and soul are two inseparable constituents of what a person is— combined they make for a "psycho-somatic" unity. In this view, it is not possible for me to say that I have a certain soul, but the "wrong" body. Therefore, there is no such thing as a female soul trapped in a male body, or reversed.

Yet, the dualism of Gnostics and Cartesians has left its dangerous imprints in the gender debate. On the one side there are those who claim that "gender" has everything to do with body parts, so male parts mean you're a boy while female parts mean you're a girl. Just ask the delivery room nurse. However, we need to be careful with this identification. What about hermaphrodites who have both male and female body parts? And what about men or women who tragically lost their "distinctively" male or female body parts? Do we say to a woman who has lost her breasts to a radical mastectomy that she is less of a woman? Gender is more than a mere collection of body parts. Yet, your body is an essential part of who you are, otherwise you could use it however you want, as if it were only a tool.

The other side of the debate says that the body has nothing whatsoever to do with sex and gender—that sex and gender are nothing more than a social, cultural, or psychological construction. The only question for such people then is, according to David Carlin, who gets to do the "constructing." There has indeed always been a lot of "constructing" in terms of gender. In certain cultures, once originated in Persia, males wear trousers, whereas tunics and robes are more typical among Muslims and ancient Greeks or Romans. Traditionally, females have usually worn skirts and robes, but nowadays they increasingly wear jeans.

Earrings are common among females in our culture, but they are now also popular among some males. The army used to be for males, but in many countries it is now open to females. Firefighting is no longer an exclusively masculine activity, and nursing is no longer an entirely feminine activity. The list could go on and on. The only boundary that cannot be crossed is the child-bearing capacity of females. No "constructing" there! Our bodies contain a self-sufficient digestive or respiratory system, but it only contains half of a reproductive system, and thus must be paired with a half-system belonging to a person of the opposite sex in order to carry out its function. In other words, gender may be pliable, but sex is not.

One of the problems genderism creates is that it actually blurs the distinction between sex and gender. Just as it considers gender to be a social construct, it also tends to see sex as a social construct, or at least as something in the minds of people who think that their bodies are in reality of the opposite sex. This certainly obscures the fact that sex is something determined at the moment of conception by the presence or absence of the Y-chromosome. Although, technically speaking, it is not the Y chromosome but rather the *SRY* gene on the Y chromosome that determines maleness, it is still fair to say that being male or female was determined at the moment the Y-chromosome entered the egg-cell during fertilization.

But after that, other factors come into play shaping the gender of a person of a certain sex. There seems to be an extended process that runs from genes to sex, and from sex to gender. Apparently, the gender of a person is much farther away from a person's genes than the sex of a person. On the "way" to gender, there are many inroads from the environment—hormones, the impact of upbringing, peers, and cultural expectations. This may partly explain why girls can

106

differ in femininity and boys in masculinity. Whereas sex differences are "inborn," gender differences appear to be more "acquired," "taught," or even "self-taught." When growing up, we often follow habits acquired at home, in school, through peers and friends, and through the society we live in—and all of these help shape our gender. This is not to say that gender has nothing to do with genes, but gender, more often than not, may be a matter of lifestyle choices rather than the outcome of a set of genetic instructions.

However, the "typical" boy, with his more advanced spatial skills, may well prefer activities like climbing, or pushing trucks around—all of which further sharpen his visual-spatial skills. The "typical" girl, by contrast, may gravitate more toward games with dolls and siblings, which further reinforce her verbal and social skills. On the other hand, this does not mean there are wonderful opportunities to compensate for the different "tendencies" of boys and girls. But it is nonsense to demand that dolls should be given to boys also. That is probably not helping their identity; we should rather confirm their given identity.

The point is not to discourage children from sex-typical play, but we may want to supplement those activities with experiences that encourage the development of a wider range of capabilities, without confusing them. Gender is just a further implementation of the finer details of a person's given sex and personality. It allows for a broader scale, albeit within the dichotomy of the two sexes. The gender of members of the female sex can be feminine to different degrees, while the gender of those of the male sex can be masculine to different degrees. In the meantime, the dichotomy of male and female remains standing.

The problem for the doctrine of genderism is, though, that persons whose biological identity is male cannot have a female gender identity; if they think they do, it is only in their minds as an imitation of the other sex. Sexual orientation is not a social construction but a biological one that is essential to our identity. That is an undeniable biological fact, which is an essential part of our sexual identity. When two people with same-sex attraction live together, one of them usually plays the male role while the other plays the female role—but these roles are obviously social roles, not sexual roles, or perhaps gender roles at best.

This takes us to another problem that genderism has to face: How could we ever change someone's sex? How could I ever say that I have a soul imprisoned in the wrong body, and therefore need sex-change surgery? As Randall Smith put it, "Only a man missing a foot who accidentally picked up the wrong artificial foot at the hospital can truly say: 'I have the wrong foot.' But a man cannot look at his own living foot and say: 'I have the wrong foot.' Still less can he look at his own body in the mirror and say: 'I have the wrong body.'" This is certainly a serious problem for genderism.

Genderism talks about the body as something we "own"— and therefore can manipulate the way we desire. However, when we say we "have" a body, we are not talking in terms of ownership. We can't even say "I have a foot"—only a person with a prosthesis can say that. In a similar way, says Randall Smith, "I do not *own* my body; it is *my* body in the sense that it is a part of *me*." This brings us to the core of transgender surgery.

True, if the human body were merely a machine, without a soul, mind, or spirit, we could alter the body in surgery and "fix" it as we would fix a car or an appliance. For many people today, the human body belongs to a person who "owns" it as property. Thus, the human body becomes an object—a thing that is owned, like a machine. If the human body were indeed a machine, and not the expression of a human person, many things would be possible. For example, we could rent it out, as in prostitution; we could claim it, as in rape; and we could change its sex, as in transgender surgery.

This belies the plain fact, however, that persons whose biological sex is male cannot have a female gender identity; if they think they do, it is only an imitation of their personal conception of the other sex. Genderism destroys a person's identity as a man or a woman. It obscures the reality of sex differences, making us believe that we can manipulate sex differences entirely to our own liking. It gives us an alibi to reject the binary division of persons into two sexes, so that we can claim the freedom to be either, both, or neither, depending on our mood. However, the fact remains that gender does not and cannot replace or alter sex.

A person's body is a fundamental indication of what sex he or she belongs to. It is a physical, empirically verifiable reality that does not change simply because our beliefs or desires do. One can mutilate one's genitals, but one cannot change one's sex. One can change what genitalia and gonads one was born with, but not one's sex. One cannot "re-invent" oneself that way, because one never "invented" oneself to begin with. Michelle Critella M.D. makes a strong point when she says, "If I walk into my doctor's office today and say, 'Hi, I'm Margaret Thatcher,' my physician will say I am delusional and give me an anti-psychotic. Yet, if instead, I walked in and said, 'I'm a man,' he would say, 'Congratulations, you're transgender.'"

That's when some people ask for sex-change surgery. However, receiving hormones of the opposite sex and having genitalia or gonads surgically removed or replaced are not sufficient to change one's sex. In 1979, after commissioning a study of the outcomes of sex-change operations, Dr. Paul McHugh in his capacity as chair of the Department of Psychiatry, put a halt to transsexual surgery at Johns

Hopkins Hospital. He wrote, "We psychiatrists, I thought, would do better to concentrate on trying to fix their minds and not their genitalia." McHugh compares medical treatment of patients who have a confused gender identity to treating anorexia with liposuction. He calls transgendered individuals "feminized men or masculinized women, counterfeits or impersonators of the sex with which they 'identify.'"

We must come to the conclusion that gender does not replace sex, nor does it nullify sex. Gender is a social construct placed on a biological foundation. That's not what genderism wants us to believe, though. Gender-identity is now seen as depending on how children want to define "their sexual reality." They are who they say they are, if they say so. However, "feelings" cannot negate the verdict rendered by the chromosomes found in every single cell of the body. In other words, biological reality cannot be replaced or overwritten by some social construct. We cannot change reality by imagining that we are what we say we are. Instead, we must acknowledge that sex is not a social construction but a biological one that we are born with.

But there are other problems with genderism. This doctrine is steered more by an ideological bias than by medical research. The idealized picture genderism portrays of gender dysphoria and sex-change surgery is not too encouraging. A 2015 study found that 180 transsexual teenagers (106 female-to-male; 74 male-to-female) had a twofold to threefold increase in risk of psychiatric disorders, including depression, anxiety, suicidal ideation, suicide attempts, self-harm without lethal intent, and both inpatient and outpatient mental health treatment compared to a control group.

A recent report by Dr. Lawrence Mayer and Dr. Paul McHugh, based on nearly 200 peer-reviewed studies of sexual orientation and gender identity, discloses some striking information. First, only a minority of children who express gender-atypical thoughts or behavior will continue to do so into adolescence or adulthood. Second, among transgender individuals, 41% have attempted suicide, whereas only 4.6% of the overall U.S. population reports "a lifetime suicide attempt." The hypothesis of "social stress" as an explanation has so far not been corroborated. Third, one hospital's practice of surgically removing the poorly-developed genitalia of male infants and giving them female genitalia showed that, years later, most of the subjects still identified as male, although their parents had been directed to raise the boys as girls.

An added problem of genderism is that it tries to replace reality with a make-believe version of it. However, perception does not change reality. Think of this comparison. The situation of trans-*sexual* individuals comes close to the position of trans-*racial* individuals. There are many similarities. If you can be transgender, why can't you be transracial? In either case, there is a *decision* to changeover. We had a recent case of someone who claimed a "transracial identity," in a way similar to claims of a transsexual identity. This sparked a conversation that we did not even know we needed to have. Is it really possible for an individual to be born "in the wrong skin"? There is that soul-body separation again. Even if you identify closely with the Black community, that does not make you a person of African descent.

Something similar could be said about transsexual or transgender individuals. In either case, proponents of transition are quick to claim that they want to redefine "traditional labels" of sexuality, inspiring some to do the same with ethnicity. Yet perception does not change reality. Just as transgendered men do not become women, or do transgendered women become men—for our sex is part of who we are—in a similar way do transracial individuals not become members of another race by perception, because their skin color, for instance, is a part of who they are. A woman declaring that she is a man is just as odd as a white woman declaring that she is "actually" black.

But there are more problems with genderism. One of them is that it gets caught in its own contradictions, which makes it a self-defeating doctrine. For instance, it speaks of gender stereotyping when people say that boys like to play with guns, but then it uses the stereotype it rejects by asserting that a girl playing with guns must actually be a boy. Thus it reinforces the gender stereotypes it claims to be rejecting.

Another contradiction of the gender ideology is that, in essence, it rejects the very gender concept they swear by. For instance, people who are willing to go through all the extensive procedures of a sex-change are basically telling us that gender apparently is not simply what someone perceives it to be. As noted by Joseph Backholm, "You can't become a woman if being a woman doesn't mean something and the moment you try to switch your gender, you are acknowledging that male and female are distinct." That's quite a self-defeating strategy.

But the trouble for genderism doesn't end here. In essence, it rejects the very gender concept it was built on. At its most basic level, the gender concept simply asserts that "sex" and "gender" are not identical. But then, gender ideologists reject that very distinction. They decided— sometimes openly, sometimes slyly—to change the definition of the gender concept by redefining "gender" to refer to the sex a person identifies with. So sex and gender are no longer different—a biological concept, sex, versus a social construct, gender. They both have been equated to a social construct.

The irony of all of this is that genderism creates a new

form of discrimination: It discriminates on the basis of and in favor of gender identity. As Edward Whelan, President of the Ethics and Public Policy Center, puts it, "It makes gender identity determine which restrooms and showers a person is allowed to use, just as a policy of race segregated restrooms and showers makes race determine which facilities a person is allowed to use." And then he asks, "How could one of the males be allowed to use the girls' facilities and the other be barred from doing so?" If transgender people truly want "equal protection under the law," they cannot expect to be treated as a separate class of people, distinct from the rest of society. That's basically a form of sectarianism— a form of bigotry, discrimination, or hatred arising from differences between subdivisions within a group.

Some side effects of Genderism

What makes the doctrine or ideology of genderism even more dangerous is that it affects adolescents during the time they are still very malleable, susceptible, and impressionable. Dr. Paul Hruz, a pediatric endocrinologist, says about them, "Young people constitute a singularly vulnerable group and experience high rates of depression, self-harm, and even suicide. Moreover, children are not fully capable of understanding what it means to be a man or a woman."

Why is that, you might ask. The main reason is that the prefrontal cortex—the part of the brain that enables us to assess situations, make sound decisions, and keep our emotions and desires under control—is still maturing during adolescence. Adolescence is a time for rapid cognitive development. It is a stage of life in which the individual's thoughts start taking more of an abstract form, whereas egocentric thoughts decrease. This allows the individual to think and reason in a wider context, thanks to cognitive skills that enable the control and coordination of thoughts and behavior. The thoughts, ideas, and concepts developed during this period of life greatly influence one's future life, playing a major role in character and personality formation. No wonder, some of us consider this period from birth to adolescence to be a major factor to shape the rest of our lives.

There is no specific age at which the adolescent brain becomes an adult brain. Structures responsible for logical reasoning mature on average by the time people are 16 years old, but structures involved in self-regulation are still developing in young adulthood. This is why 16-year-olds are just as competent as adults when it comes to granting informed medical consent, but still immature in ways that diminish their criminal responsibility, as the Supreme Court has noted in several recent cases. Using different ages for different legal boundaries may seem odd, but it would make some neuro-scientific sense. That's why there are age restrictions on voting, for instance. However, reality is that age boundaries are drawn for mainly political reasons, not scientific ones.

The fact that a crucial part of the brain is still a work-in-progress during adolescence puts adolescents at a higher risk for making poor decisions (such as experimenting with drugs) and for exposure to ideologies (such a genderism). This makes it rather dangerous to indoctrinate and sway adolescents with a dangerous ideology, especially genderism. Now that the pediatric mantra has become "helping kids transition from one gender to another," one should wonder whether this is really the best way of helping them.

It is interesting to note that many in the medical community have been indoctrinated by scientism (see Chapter 12) and therefore feverishly try to explain that helping kids with sex-change transition is demanded by science. Instead of acknowledging the scientific facts about brain maturing, they decided to replace the longstanding diagnosis of "gender identity disorder" with "gender dysphoria." Well, if there is no longer any "disorder" to treat psychiatrically, the proper course necessarily becomes mutilation—via hormones and surgery. However, in going down that road, one invalidates the entire concept of psychiatric disorder so that no one at all could ever be deemed delusional. By saying this, the American Psychiatric Association (APA) is, unwittingly, trying to put itself out of business. If the reality is what we want it to be, that would be the end of medical science.

The physician and philosopher Carl Elliott, MD, was right when he said that cultural and historical conditions have not just revealed transsexuals, but may actually be creating them. Unfortunately, psychiatrists have powerful voices in this discussion. They have taken on the "authority" to decide whether the transgender issue is "real." They are supposed to speak in the name of science, making many people bow their heads in obedience. However, the problem with psychiatry is that its practitioners often try to disguise their personal convictions and opinions as scientific facts. Psychiatry is arguably the least science-based branch of the medical specialties; some experts do not even consider it a science. It is very susceptible to philosophical, ideological, and religious viewpoints—probably because its field of study is very close to those territories. Because of this affinity, it exposes itself easily to contamination, and thus to criticism.

Right or not, the psychiatrist Thomas Szasz goes as far as rejecting the whole concept of mental illness; he considers it a plot to interfere with a person's human rights—a "science of lies," as he calls it. Nevertheless, all professionals in mental health in general, and psychiatry in particular, should take the time to look at their own preconceptions, actions, statements, and morals. It is frightening to see how much decisive power psychiatrists have been given in our healthcare system and judicial system. But if we feel ourselves to be at their mercy, that is something we bring on ourselves.

It is also to be expected that genderism has had a devastating impact on religion. No wonder the Catholic Church has mentioned this issue repeatedly in recent years. In 2012, Pope Benedict XVI connected an extreme version of the gender theory with the words of the French philosopher Simone de Beauvoir: "one is not born a woman, one becomes so"—in denial of the fact that one is born as a woman, but may not think so. Taken this way, the pontiff declared the "gender" ideology a new philosophy of sexuality: "According to this philosophy, sex is no longer a given element of nature, that man has to accept and personally make sense of: it is a social role that we choose for ourselves, while in the past it was chosen for us by society." The Pontiff was basically asserting that this version of gender theory confuses sex with gender, and thus confuses sexual identity with gender identity.

Instead, it must be stated that sexual identity refers to *being* male or female. In the words of the Catechism (2333), "Everyone, man and woman, should acknowledge and accept his sexual identity." So we need to unite body and soul again by being happy in our bodies. The Catechism (2393) states, "By creating the human being man and woman, God gives personal dignity equally to the one and the other. Masculinity and femininity are complementary—different but equal expressions of what it is to be human. Each of them, man and woman, should acknowledge and accept his sexual identity." Interestingly enough, it was through each other that Adam and Eve discovered their own identity, in body and soul.

Given all of the above, we must come to the conclusion that genderism is a doctrine which is not only seriously flawed but also very destructive.

8. Communism

What is Communism?

The term "Communism" as we use it in this chapter covers a number of closely related doctrines ranging from Marxism to Communism to Socialism. What unites them is a rejection of Capitalism (see Chapter 9). What divides them is much harder to define, because there are several variants of each. But let's try.

In political circles and regular conversation, people often use the terms "Marxism," "Socialism," and "Communism" interchangeably, as if these three doctrines are the same. However, they do have important distinctions. Marxism is the theoretical framework which lays the foundation for the economic and political doctrines of Socialism and Communism.

Marxism believes that workers, under the capitalist system of government, have sold their labor and that this labor has become a commodity. This commodity has gained a surplus value for the capitalist, but not for the worker, which creates an inherent conflict between the working class and the ownership class. This is where class warfare starts.

Socialism advocates more and more public ownership of property and natural resources rather than private owner-ship. The socialist system of government values cooperation over the competitiveness of a free-market economy. Social-ists believe that all people in society contribute to the production of goods and services and that those goods should be shared. Its main goal is narrowing, not totally eliminating, the gap between the rich and the poor. It calls for putting the major means of production in the hands of the people, either directly or through the government. Socialism also believes that wealth and income should be shared more equally among people. The government has a responsibility to re-distribute wealth to make society more fair and just.

Communism differs from the socialist worldview because it calls not only for public ownership of property and natural resources, but also for public ownership of the means of pro-duction of goods and services. The most important principle of communism is that no private ownership of property should be allowed. Its goal is to eliminate the gap between the rich and poor and thus bring about economic equality. Property should be divided and shared, and the people or the state should ultimately control the economy.

What is wrong with Communism?

The Catholic Church rejects the doctrine of communism, in all its three forms, for very fundamental reasons.

One of those reasons is that Communism glorifies society over individuals. However, no matter how long we search around us, going from person to person, we will never come across a society. Looking around in our surroundings, we do not perceive a society but only human beings—individual human beings, that is. So we should learn from this that the individuals are the sole full reality in society. Society only exists by virtue of its individuals.

Communism, in contrast, takes the opposite view: society is the one and only real entity, at the "cost" of individuals. Consequently, the individuals are seen only as parts of a lar-ger whole—as termites in a colony, so to speak—and therefore do not qualify as complete entities. Just like the hand of a person is not complete in itself, but only a part of the person, in the same way an individual person only exists as part of society. As a consequence, individuals have no rights and duties of their own. After all, they live their lives as part of society, through the power of society, and for the benefit of society. The result is some kind of socio-ethical collectivism, ranging from authoritarianism (in which a single power monopolizes all personal and social power) to totalitarianism (in which the regime attempts to control virtually all aspects of personal and social life). What both doctrines have in common is that they turn citizens into a mere means for the sole purpose of advancing society—in the same way as ants and bees only exist to keep the colony alive.

But at the very moment we glorify the "colony" over its "members," individuals lose all their rights and become mere slaves of the totality—which leads to various kinds of pure totalitarianism. However, it is persons who have rights, society doesn't. Not surprisingly, the Church explicitly rejects, in the words of the Catechism (2425), "the totalitarian and atheistic ideologies associated in modem times with 'communism' or 'socialism.'" The horrors placed on human beings by totalitarian regimes—in the labor camps run by Nazis, Soviets, and Maoists, for instance—tell us how ugly this ideology can get. It can easily turn a society of human beings into a colony of termites or bees. As Pope Pius XI put it in a nutshell, "Society is for man, not vice versa." When Pope John Paul II issued *Centesimus Annus* in 1991, he diagnosed the root problem as follows: "Socialism considers the individual person simply as an element, a molecule within the social organism, so that the good of the individual is completely subordinated to the functioning of the socio-economic mechanism."

On the other hand, it is obvious that society is more than

a mere collection of individuals, more than the sum total of its individuals. We are not like gas molecules that bounce into each other at random. The reason for that is very simple: we are *social* beings. We are not born as citizens but as sons and daughters in a family. Since humans are fundamentally social beings, rather than individualists, they have a natural tendency to create organizations beyond the individual— which are structures that range from nuclear families, extended families, and clans to cities, states, tribes, organizations, civilizations, cultures, and societies. In this Catholic view, the society is more than the sum total of its individual members, with all of them having their own positions, responsibilities, and relationships within a larger entity—society.

In this view, society is not merely some kind of organization but rather something like an *organism*, in which the individual parts work together in harmony. Since human beings have a natural aptitude to live in society with others, they cannot attain their well-being outside of society. When one member is afflicted, all the others are affected. This calls for mutual responsibility and solidarity. In other words, living in society is not a pragmatic arrangement, but an intrinsically necessity for human beings. As St. Paul worded it, "The eye cannot say to the hand, 'I have no need of you,' nor again the head to the feet, 'I have no need of you'" (1 Cor. 12:21).

The second reason for questioning Communism follows from the previous one. In glorifying society over individuals, Communism is a threat to the human dignity of each individual. As said earlier, individuals have rights, society doesn't. Individuals have rights such as the right to life, liberty, and the pursuit of happiness as stated in the United States Declaration of Independence (see Chapter 6), but they also have the right of private property. You and I are not a quantity or statistic, but we have a precious quality—the quality of being made in God's image and likeness. The Christian basis for property rights lies in the fact that man is created in the image of God, and that is where our human dignity and human rights stem from—and no society can take those away.

In 1891, Pope Leo XIII issued his encyclical *Rerum Novarum* [On New Things] in which he also touched on the notion of private property: "To remedy these wrongs the socialists, working on the poor man's envy of the rich, are striving to do away with private property." This, he declared, is "emphatically unjust," and the "remedy they propose is manifestly against justice. For, every man has by nature the right to possess private property as his own." Regarding the role of private property, Leo insists, "The first and most fundamental principle, therefore, if one would undertake to alleviate the condition of the masses, must be the inviolability of private property." The pontiff sought a Christian basis for property rights in the fact that man is created in the image of God. Needless to say that the Church also admits that a person may lawfully abandon this property right; but she denies that humans can be forced to do so.

Communism, in contrast, wants to redistribute property by taking it from the rich and giving it to the poor. Private ownership is supposed to be replaced by public ownership so that everything is owned by the collective all. Doing so amounts to coveting, a violation of the ninth and tenth Commandments. Pope Leo's encyclical *Rerum Novarum* pointed this out: "The authority of the divine law adds its sanction, forbidding us in severest terms even to covet that which is another's." In addition, Communism is built upon the false idea of class warfare. Here too, Pope Leo dismissed "the notion that class is naturally hostile to class, and that the wealthy and the working men are intended by nature to live in mutual conflict. So irrational and so false is this view that the direct contrary is the truth."

The third reason for rejecting Communism is that it overestimates the role of the state. Only in totalitarian countries is society identical to the state. As we said before, society is certainly not identical to the state nor its government—society is all of us together. In line with Thomas Aquinas, the Catholic Church sees the government as an aid to work for the "common good"—that is, to the benefit of all. She does not take the common good in an individualistic way—as the sum total of every person's self-interest bumping up against everyone else's self-interest, with the government serving as the referee. Neither does she understand the common good in a totalitarian way as whatever is best for the state is best for all. Neither does she take it as the greatest possible good for the greatest possible number of individuals, which would be too bad for the people who are not included in "the greatest possible number."

So what then can the state do for society? Pope Leo XIII makes very clear that it's the role of the State to promote social justice through the protection of individual rights, while the Church must speak out on social issues in order to teach correct social principles and ensure class harmony. He defends the basic rights of the individual and the family and their priority with regard to the State. Therefore, he warns against excessive state economic intervention, especially against efforts to replace the Church's charitable and anti-poverty work with government agencies.

How can this be done? In answering this question, Pope Leo had to carefully navigate between the Scylla of Capitalism and the Charybdis of Communism. So in his encyclical *Rerum novarum*, he introduced into Catholic social thought the concept of *subsidiarity*, the principle that political and social decisions should be made at a local level, if possible, rather than by a central authority at a state level. With this principle, Leo made an attempt to articulate a middle course between Capitalism, promoting a laissez-faire policy controlled by individuals, and Communism, which subordinates the individual to the state. Subsidiarity locates the responsibilities and privileges of social life in the smallest unit of organization at which they function best. Subsidiarity calls for simple, local problem-solving whenever possible. Things are best done, in other words, at the smallest appropriate scale. Larger social bodies, be they the state or otherwise, are permitted and required to intervene only when smaller ones cannot carry out these tasks themselves.

The fourth reason for rejecting Communism is its atheism (see Chapter 15). According to many experts, all the previous reasons are based on what is at the root of Communism: atheism, wrapped up in materialism (see Chapter 10). The fact is that Communism focuses exclusively on the material conditions of life—bread for the masses. Communism had made this very point the core of its promise of "salvation": see to it that no one goes hungry anymore. But the Communist salvation is only technically and materially based, so its remedies merely give us stones in place of bread. In response, the Church would say, human beings have *two* sides—a material one and a spiritual one. Humans don't live on bread alone.

Later, in 1931, Pope Pius XI released *Quadragesimo Anno* in which he stated bluntly: "We make this pronouncement: Whether considered as a doctrine, or an historical fact, or a movement, socialism... is utterly foreign to Christian truth." The pontiff went further stating: "If socialism, like all errors, contains some truth, it is based nevertheless on a theory of human society peculiar to itself and irreconcilable with true Christianity. Religious socialism,

Christian socialism, are contradictory terms; no one can be at the same time a good Catholic and a true socialist." Pope John XXIII would later reiterate this point in his 1961 encyclical *Mater et Magistra* saying "Pope Pius XI further emphasized the fundamental opposition between communism and Christianity, and made it clear that no Catholic could subscribe even to moderate socialism."

Why is Communism bound to fail? As Bishop Fulton Sheen wisely observed, "Communism tries to establish the impossible: a brotherhood of man without a fatherhood of God." Human Equality and human rights come from God, not from Karl Marx. Nearly one-third of Pope Leo's famous 1891 encyclical *Rerum novarum* is devoted to proving that socialism does not possess the answer to the social crisis, since it would do as much harm to the workers as it might help them. He explained again the sad deficiencies of socialism—its atheistic materialism, its doctrine and practice of class-war, its denial of the rights and liberties of the human person, including the natural right to possess some measure of private property, and its contempt for good morals—and he gave an early warning of the misery it would inflict on the world. His words would turn out to be highly prophetic.

Some side effects of Communism

In spite of the incompatibility between Communism and Christianity, Communism has been able to infiltrate Christianity, its archenemy, with what has become known as *Liberation Theology*. Its core message is that the Church should act to bring about social change, and ally itself with the working class and the poor to accomplish their goals. This message, in turn, led to a movement of radical priests in the middle of the previous century—so-called "worker priests"—becoming involved in politics and trade unions while still others aligned themselves with violent revolutionary movements. But John Paul II who had long understood the deceits of Marxism, Communism, and Socialism, saw Liberation Theology more clearly as a fusion of Christianity and Marxism and responded by closing institutions that taught the ideology and removed or rebuked the movement's activists, such as Leonardo Boff and Gustavo Gutierrez.

There is nothing wrong with the "liberation" part of "Liberation Theology." Liberation had always been a traditional Catholic notion; it meant liberating people from those moral deficiencies that prevent one from pleasing God and attaining eternal life. But that is not what the new liberators meant. The term "liberation," the way the Liberation Theology understands it, is closer to the word "liberation" in the Chinese Liberation army than in the Biblical liberation that comes through grace. What the "new liberators" had in mind was a freeing from economic poverty and political oppression, more in specific the political domination by the capitalism of the United States. Liberation Theology is in essence Marxist "theology," proclaiming poor people as good, and rich people as bad.

The core problem of Liberation Theology is that its basic focal point is not God, but "the people," more in particular the "oppressed people"—at best the "people of God," which is that famous phrase borrowed from the Second Vatican Council. However, what the Council really said is that this "People" were to be led by the Roman Pontiff and the bishops in communion with that Pontiff—and not by their own instincts or by the social theory of Karl Marx. In contrast, the battle that Liberation Theology wants its devotees to fight and to win is a class warfare—a worldwide battle against the toils and traps of the rich. These new liberators were giving the term *poor* the same meaning as Marx and Marxists had given to the term *proletariat.*

Closely connected with this new liberation ideology is the concept of *social justice.* The term itself is not new either, but was introduced by Pope Pius XI into Catholic teaching in his 1923 encyclical *Studiorum Ducem,* and then was used extensively in two later encyclicals. One thing is clear in these cases, social justice has little or nothing to do with "redistribution of wealth by a government"; it has nothing to do with "taking from the rich and giving to the poor." The "poor" in the Bible are first of all "poor in spirit," not "poor in means." Jesus had no preference for either rich or poor people, but he did have a preference for the "poor in spirit" who know they are in need of redemption.

Of course, social justice is and will always continue to be part of Catholic doctrine. The issue of social justice is addressed, among other places, in the Catechism of the Catholic Church (1929): "Social justice can be obtained only in respecting the transcendent dignity of man. The person represents the ultimate end of society, which is ordered to him: What is at stake is the dignity of the human person, whose defense and promotion have been entrusted to us by the Creator, and to whom the men and women at every moment of history are strictly and responsibly in debt." Combating all causes of unjust inequalities, which especially affect the poor, if understood properly, is indeed a path to a truly liberated and more just society.

A good example of social justice understood properly can be found in the work of Mother Teresa of Calcutta, who wanted her Missionaries of Charity to focus on the immediate needs of the poor, that is, feeding them and tending to their health. That is social justice optima forma. She was sometimes criticized for not challenging the social structures that made people poor in the first place. Her response was: "That's not what we're about!"

Like Mother Teresa, Karl Marx may have been moved by the harsh conditions of workers, but unlike Mother Teresa, all Marx proposed were alternative ideas about ownership and government—and not very good ones at that, as it turned out. There was no guarantee (except in his mind) that Marx's ideas would lead to the "progress" that he envisaged. Forcing the complex dynamics of the world to fit his misconceptions caused the deaths of tens of millions in the name of progress in countries such as China and the Soviet Union. Yet surveys show that many philosophy departments in America still teach Marxism as a serious, honorable subject. Winston Churchill may be very right: "Those who fail to learn from history are doomed to repeat it."

Given all of the above, we must come to the conclusion that Communism is a doctrine which is not only seriously flawed but also very destructive.

9. Capitalism

What is Capitalism?

Like a handful of similar words in contemporary social and political discourse—such as secularism, humanism, liberalism, rights and religion—the term capitalism has come to mean a lot of different things to a lot of different people. When people hear the word "capitalism," many of them think "entrepreneurship, commerce, innovation and technological progress, private property." Who would not approve these things! Others, however, hear "greed, materialism, cut-throat competition, exploitation of workers." Who would not condemn those things! In reality, like basically every human endeavor, capitalism as currently practiced contains a mixture of praiseworthy and damnable behavior.

So we need to start with separating "the good and the bad." When discussing the doctrine of Capitalism, we should distinguish at least two very different meanings of the term— an economic one and a philosophical one. The economic meaning is rather straightforward: an economy based on the law of supply and demand. The philosophical meaning—very different from the economic one—is in essence a form of *individualism*, which could be characterized as the antithesis of Communism in the sense of *collectivism*. Let's discuss them separately, beginning with the economic version.

In this interpretation, capitalism is basically just a system or model of economic activities. It is a form of capitalism that is based on private ownership of the means of production and on individual economic freedom. The means of production, such as factories and businesses, are owned by private individuals. Private owners make decisions about what and when to produce and how much products should cost. And private buyers decide what to buy and what not to buy. A market is a place where buyers and sellers come together to engage in economic exchanges.

This is an idealized model of economic capitalism, which is often referred to as "free-market" economy. In a free-market economy, prices for goods and services are set freely. "Free" means there is no intervention from outside forces such as governments or any other outside powers. It does not mean, however, that sellers are "free" to set any price they want or that employers are "free" to set wages for labor at any level they want. A "free-market" only means that producers are free to enter a line of business and sell their products at whatever price they can charge; meanwhile consumers are free to buy whatever products they want at whatever price they are willing to accept.

The mechanism behind this process is supposed to follow the law or principle of "supply and demand," which is an economic model of determining prices in a market. In theory, prices will be kept as low as possible because consumers will seek the best product for the least amount of money. In a free-market system, prices are determined by how many products there are and how many people want them. When supplies increase, prices tend to drop. If prices drop, demand usually increases until supplies run out. Then prices will rise once more, but only as long as demand is high. The principle of supply and demand works in a cycle to control prices and keep them from getting too high or too low.

The same principle can also be applied to wages in the labor market. But now the typical roles of supplier and consumer are reversed. The suppliers are individuals who try to sell (supply) their labor for the highest price. The consumers are businesses who try to buy (demand) the type of labor they need at the lowest price. The principle of supply and demand works here too in a cycle to control wages and keep them from getting too high or too low. By the forces of supply and demand, both prices of products and wages of laborers are supposed to reach their point of equilibrium without intervention by the government. In theory, everybody in a capitalistic, free-market economy has the right to engage in exchanges or not to engage in exchanges.

On the other hand, it is only in an idealized free-market economy that prices for goods and services are set freely by the forces of supply and demand and are allowed to reach their point of equilibrium without intervention by government policy. Indeed, the government generally does not set the prices of goods or the wages of labor—the market sets those. This is in contrast with a regulated market, in which a government intervenes in supply and demand through various methods such as discriminatory taxes, subsidies, tariffs, or minimum wages—all being used to regulate trade and protect the economy. Nowadays, in most economies, markets are regulated to some extent by the government. But it is still capitalism in the economic sense, albeit not completely of the free-market type.

In addition there is also a form of capitalism with a strong philosophical dimension—which might better be called "individualism." As we discussed in the previous chapter, when looking around in our community, we perceive only human beings—individual human beings, that is. Such considerations have persuaded certain philosophers and sociologists to voice the view that "society" is a pure fiction. They take it that only individual persons exist in reality—a collection of autonomous, pure egos without any ties or connections. Some call this the Crusoe model of an "isolated man face-to-face with nature." It is individualism optima forma.

The viewpoint of pure individualism has in fact only very few proponents, except in a mitigated way. Thomas Hobbes, Adam Smith, Max Weber, and more currently F. A. von Hayek and Karl Popper are individualists, at least in a methodological sense, because they think of individualism as the key principle about how to practice social science and economics. Ayn Rand, who promoted the "virtue of selfishness" as well as a form of laissez-faire capitalism, could probably be considered an individualist in this sense too. Another representative, Ludwig von Mises of the Austrian School of economics, would also argue that only individuals act, and that society does not exist apart from the thoughts and actions of individuals, since society is supposedly nothing more than people trying to achieve their own individual interests. This view of society "atomizes" society, so that the single individuals bounce into each other just like atoms and molecules in gases do. It leads to what Thomas Hobbes described as "war of all against all" and causes a man to be "a wolf to his fellow man."

What is wrong with Capitalism?

What is the Church's position in this debate? When we want to ask about the pros and cons of Capitalism, and what is wrong with it, we should always begin our answer this way: "Well, if by capitalism you mean..."—otherwise we end up in an endless and fruitless discussion.

Well, there is probably not much wrong with Capitalism if it is only understood as a free-market economic system.

Characteristics central to this form of Capitalism include private property, capital accumulation, wage labor, voluntary exchange, a price system, and competitive markets. The Catholic Church does not really reject Capitalism in the sense of a free-market economy. Pope Leo XIII could not have said it more forcefully, "Capital needs labor and labor needs capital."

There is nothing wrong with "capital" or "money" either. St. Paul is often incorrectly cited as saying that "money is the root of all evil." On the contrary, what he condemned was attachment to money that's excessive: "For the love of money is a root of all kinds of evil, and in their eagerness to be rich some have wandered away from the faith and pierced themselves with many pains" (1 Tim. 6:20). The problem is not money; it is attachment to money. This shifts the focus to "greed" in a free-market economy. However, greed was already a deadly sin long before the invention of free-market capitalism. Free enterprise is not another word for greed. Free enterprise is not the culprit—it has brought so much good to billions of people.

There is nothing wrong with making money, unless it is driven by mere greed. There is nothing wrong with owning private property, unless it is stolen. There is nothing wrong with buying and selling, as long as the price benefits both parties equally. There is nothing wrong with trading goods for a profit, as long as the profit is in proportion to the good traded and the risks taken. There is nothing wrong with having people work for you, as long as you pay them fairly and treat them decently. There is nothing wrong with being an employer, nor with being an employee, as long as they respect each other's role and position in the economy. There is nothing wrong with investing or borrowing money, as long as the interest is fair. There is nothing wrong with charging interest on borrowed money, as long as the lender takes some risk in the transaction.

Although there is nothing intrinsically wrong with economic capitalism, not even free-market capitalism, serious problems do arise when free-market capitalism teams up with individualism. So, instead of asking "What is wrong with Capitalism?" we should rather pose the question "What is wrong with Individualism?" Well, then, what is the problem of individualism?

The main problem of individualism is that it sees society as a mere collection of isolated individuals, who never really interact with each other. If they seem to interact, it's not really an interaction—but at best a struggle for survival: the survival of the fittest who survives at the cost of others. This view assesses everything in terms of "winners" and "losers"—only the "fittest" are supposed to survive at the cost of the weakest. It is about success at the *expense* of others—never about duties to the *benefit* of others. Speaking in terms of a "survival battle" makes all individuals serve their own individual "interest." No wonder, the "master" comes out as the winner, leaving the "worker" behind as the loser. This way we do end up in a class warfare.

Individualism sees society simply as a combination of individuals, each with their own self-interests. This view leads to what some call "Crusoe Economics." A close representative of this view is Adam Smith who considered society as being guided by an "invisible hand." When no central planning is in place, there is no one entity which controls the workings of the entire market. Yet, trends and patterns emerge. Although individuals always act in their own self-interest, the surprising result is that society benefits, and no government action is needed to insure that the public interest is promoted. Private greed leads somehow to public benefit, says Smith paradoxically. Can that be true?

What has gotten lost in this view is that we are *social*

beings who need others for our wellbeing—"I" is part of "We." We are not born as individuals but as sons and daughters in a family. Everyone's life has a totally public character because individuals can be defined only through their membership in the social whole of society. In other words, there are not only "individual goods and interests," but there is also a "common good and interest." In a culture of individualism, the very notion of the common good has become increasingly unthinkable. It is more and more thought of as nothing more than the aggregate sum of individual goods: the more fun I have, the more I add to the aggregate sum; the richer I am, the more I add to the aggregate sum. Not so, the common good is something we share with fellow citizens, so those others are not our enemies in "a war of all against all." The notion of the "common good" gives the free-market approach of capitalism a *moral* dimension, which it doesn't provide on its own.

One of the first Church leaders to see this clearly was Pope Leo XIII. He was very aware of how much the Industrial Revolution had been changing the world he saw around him. The old system of *guilds*—the socio-economic backbone of the past—was crumbling. Founded in the Middle Ages, the guilds had been social, economic, and religious all at once. Guildsmen trained the young in their trades; they maintained a high standard of quality; they provided stability in costs and profit; they cared for their invalid members and their widows and orphans; and they united in the worship of God, especially to celebrate the feasts of their patron saints. The abolition of the guilds, then, left nothing between worker and master but an empty chasm. That's what the pontiff saw missing in the new individualism of the 20th century.

Leo saw very clearly that the Industrial Revolution had opened the gate for two new ideologies: Communism and

Capitalism, with Communism focusing solely on the "worker," and Capitalism exclusively on the "master." He described the ensuing situation very aptly in one of his encyclicals: "For the result of civil change and revolution has been to divide cities into two classes separated by a wide chasm. On the one side there is the party which holds power because it holds wealth.... On the other side there is the needy and powerless multitude, sick and sore in spirit and ever ready for disturbance." He deeply felt the suffering of those who were exploited by the market or who had not been given adequate access to its benefits. They needed to be protected with political and legal reforms, including child labor laws, minimum wage requirements, anti-trust provisions, work day restrictions, the right of workers to unionize, etc. All of these legal constraints should not be construed as erosions of free-market capitalism, but rather as attempts to make it more humane, more just, and more widely accessible.

This approach puts a moral dimension into the equation. It is the tandem Capitalism-Individualism that wants the free-market to be "free," not only of governmental regulations but also of any moral restrictions. Individualism doesn't have a social and moral dimension—it is blind for the rights and obligations we have towards others; it does not acknowledge actions others owe us (our rights) and actions we owe to others (our duties). Instead, we should view individuals as members of a society—not as individuals in isolation. Because human beings are social beings, we can compare the economy to a body, in which different members serve their respective functions. Thus, it is beneficial for society to have everyone serving their own productive purpose for the community as a whole. As a consequence, once we separate the individual from the community, the common good becomes a mere aggregate of individual interests or, worse, an uneasy compromise between conflicting sets of group interests and personal values.

What is missing in this equation is a moral dimension. Therefore, Pope Pius XI pointed out that what is needed is not an excessive reaction, like Communism proposes, to destroy the whole free-market system, but rather, in his own words, the "first and most necessary remedy is a reform of morals." In a similar vein, in response to a-moral free-market extremists, Pope Benedict XVI made it very clear that "the conviction that the economy must be autonomous, that it must be shielded from 'influences' of a moral character, has led man to abuse the economic process in a thoroughly destructive way." And Pope Francis most recently followed him saying, "The service of the common good is left behind. Once capital becomes an idol and guides people's decisions, once greed for money presides over the entire socioeconomic system, it ruins society, it condemns and enslaves men and women."

The common good approach does not only apply to micro-economics but also to macro-economics at a global scale. It was Pope John Paul II who wrote in *Centesimus Annus* (1991): "It is necessary to break down the barriers and monopolies which leave so many countries on the margins of development and to provide all individuals and nations with the basic conditions which will enable them to share in development."

In other words, a market economy enjoys real legitimacy if and only if it is set in the context of a vibrant moral culture that forms its people in the virtues of fairness, justice, respect for the integrity of the other, and religion—all of which is not only a matter of self-interest but also looking out for the interests of others. Indeed, what good are contracts—fundamental to the functioning of a market economy—if people are indifferent to justice? What good is private property if people don't see that stealing is morally wrong?

To wrap up this discussion, we must conclude that the Catholic Church's stance regarding Capitalism has always been a measured approach, protecting the rights and duties of both the employer and the employee through a return to Christian morality and concern for one's neighbor. Pope John Paul II took a very cautious approach to the debate. When asked whether capitalism should be the goal of the countries now making efforts to rebuild their economy and society, his answer was twofold:

> *The answer is obviously complex. If by capitalism is meant an economic system which recognizes the fundamental and positive role of business, the market, private property and the resulting responsibility for the means of production as well as free human creativity in the economic sector, then the answer is certainly in the affirmative even though it would perhaps be more appropriate to speak of a business economy, market economy, or simply free economy.*
>
> *But if by capitalism is meant a system in which freedom in the economic sector is not circumscribed within a strong juridical framework which places it at the service of human freedom in its totality and which sees it as a particular aspect of that freedom, the core of which is ethical and religious, then the reply is certainly negative.*

Some side effects of Capitalism

In reaction to the horrifying track record of Communism—in countries such as Stalin's Soviet Union, Mao's People Republic of China, Castro's Republic of Cuba, and Chavez' socialist revolution in Venezuela—the doctrine of Capitalism has become increasingly popular and received more and more traction. But as we discussed already, it's not only Capitalism but more in particular its cousin Individualism that is becoming popular in the minds of many. Not only our economy but our entire culture has been infected by individualism.

By stating that the free-market economy has become in the grip of greed, I am not suggesting that the doctrine of individualism caused our greed. The cause-and-effect relationship is in fact reversed: greed caused the doctrine of individualism. Greed nurtured the doctrine of Individualism by making sure that individuals and their greed receive the status and authority that we usually bestow on God. So there is something much deeper and more serious going on.

Since the Fall in Paradise, we feel no longer being under the authority of God, but we have become our own authorities, not ruled by God, but controlled by our own impulses, drives, and passions—which are greed, lust, violence, extortion, and so many more vices. We no longer control them but they control us. This has happened to all aspects of life, not only in matters of economics. We consider ourselves as completely autonomous and fully in charge of ourselves (see Chapter 5).

Seen through the eyes of Individualism, society exists above all to provide for each individual's comfortable self-preservation. Any remaining notion of a common good is greatly watered down or replaced by the utilitarian ethic of "the greatest good for the greatest number of people." The focus is on safeguarding individual rights, rather than individual duties. In large-scale consumer societies, as Alexis de Tocqueville (1805-1859) predicted in his great work *Democracy in America*, individualism would become more acute and widespread. His prediction seems to have been prophetic.

Individualism is "a religion without God." It is a vision of the human person that is incomplete—it has no longer a religious dimension. This is the kind of doctrine that declares human beings to be fully sufficient in themselves, fully self-made, and in complete control of their own history. It is a philosophy of life which views man as the "supreme being" on Earth, so there is no need for, or no space left for, a Supreme Being in Heaven. It pretends that all our problems—personal, social, technological, and what have you—can be entirely solved by using the right human knowledge, technology, reasoning, and judgment. We are supposed to be in full control of ourselves and should further free ourselves through economic, technological, and social liberation—free from any moral restraints, only ruled by our own wishes, lusts, and desires. From then on, not Heaven but the sky is the limit. The slogan is: We do not need God; we do not even want God because such a god undermines the power of Man, the power of "Me, myself, and I."

Individualism puts Man, with a capital M, on center stage, without leaving any "space" for God. It features Man without a religious dimension. Man has become a solitary individual navigating on his own towards goals of his own in a society of isolated individuals. According to Pope John Paul II, people in a society of Individualism "strive for the good of man, but man who is truncated, reduced to his merely horizontal dimension." They make us believe that we are fully self-made, in full control of our own history and destination. The Man of Individualism is setting out on his own to know and master his cosmos—all of it, including his economy.

Indeed, for many people, belief in God has been replaced by Individualism, "which restricts its needs and aspirations to space and time," says the Catechism (2124). It "falsely considers man to be 'an end to himself, and the sole maker, with supreme control, of his own history'" (2124). It considers man as the "measure of all things," in spite of the religious belief that Man can only know himself in reference to God. As Pope John Paul II put it, "Without the Creator, the creature disappears." It may sound paradoxical, but it is a profound truth: When we throw God out, we throw Man out as well. No wonder then we see around us that we ignore each other, we kill each other, we cheat on each other, we betray each other, we let each other starve, we...—and the list goes on.

To counteract the doctrine of Individualism, we need things like self-control, self-denial, and self-giving. Self-giving means, in the words of Pope Benedict XVI, "stepping outside the limitations of fallen humanity—in which we are all separated from one another... stepping outside the limits of one's closed individuality." This certainly requires self-control and self-denial. The Catechism calls self-control, "a training in human freedom"; and then it goes on to say, "The alternative is clear: either man governs his passions and finds peace, or he lets himself be dominated by them and becomes unhappy" (2339). Be sure, all of this is a lifelong task and strenuous training for the "self of I."

Please do not confuse this "I" with your "Ego." Whereas "Ego" arrogantly dominates, "I" humbly reflects and corrects. In other words, "I" stands for the "transparency of the self," whereas "Ego" represents the "grandeur of the self"—something that Individualism promotes. "Ego" is self-made, self-centered, part of a so-called me-society, whereas "I" belongs

Gerard M. Verschuuren

to the "City of God." "Ego" has forgotten who "I" is. God and Ego cannot live together in the same person. As John the Baptist says about Jesus, "He must increase, but I must decrease" (John 3:30).

Who then is "I"? It is a "take-off" of Someone else, whose Name is I-AM, in whose image and likeness "I" was created. So it is our calling to determine and develop our self in line with God's image. It shouldn't surprise us then that human history since the Fall has been the opposite of this; it has mostly been a history of huge and super "Egos," a history of leaders with the biggest fangs, of cowboys with the fastest guns, of oil sheiks with the largest harems. St. Ambrose loved to say that "the great" of this world put off being humble until death humbles them." That is what happens when we confuse "I" with "Ego."

Given all of the above, we must come to the conclusion that not so much economic Capitalism itself but the tandem Capitalism-Individualism is a doctrine which is not only seriously flawed but also very destructive.

10. Materialism

What is Materialism?

There are at least two different versions of materialism. One version is about material needs and aspirations—let's call it *practical* materialism. People who are called materialistic in this sense are only interested in material benefits. The other version is about "matter" as such, in its most general sense—let's call it *philosophical* Materialism, on which we will exclusively focus in the rest of this chapter. People who are called materialistic in this second sense think about everything in terms of "matter" and explain everything in terms of "matter." The question is, of course, what they mean by "matter."

"Matter" is a very vague term that can be given almost any meaning. The concept of matter changes constantly depending on who uses the term, and it has also changed, for instance, in response to new scientific discoveries. Thus, it has become closely associated with, or for some even identical to, physicalism, which is the view that all that exists is ultimately physical. Nevertheless, the term "matter" has lost its prominent position in physics, because the term "mass" is well-defined, but "matter" is not. The nuclear physicist Werner Heisenberg, for instance, put it this way, "[A]toms are not things."

This makes the question even more pressing: What is "matter"? Let's provisionally define matter as anything that has mass and takes up space. Most people have some intuitive idea of what "matter" stands for—they probably think of it as "stuff." That's exactly where its appeal lies. The strength of materialism is that it centers on one of the most noticeable elements in the world around us—indeed, "stuff." It can usually be seen, touched, heard, tasted, and smelled by our five senses. It is everything that can be quantified, measured, counted, and dissected, particularly in science. Studying this kind of "stuff" has been vital for our survival. We cannot disregard it, we cannot live without it. It is impossible to deny that almost all our technological achievements are based on it. Where would we be without "stuff" like this?

That's probably the main reason why Materialism has become so popular. In this view, we are only able to know and study material objects that can be perceived by the five senses. Because we cannot know non-material things, so materialists say, we must conclude that non-material things do not exist and cannot exist. Their creed is, "Everything that exists is material," for nothing can exist without the materials out of which it is made. Therefore, they say, what materialism doesn't detect does not and cannot exist. This seems to be an unbeatable idea. No wonder, many people find the materialistic dogma enormously credible and even persuasive. The fact that the world we perceive through our senses and all the things we can picture are individual physical things or material embodiments gives great credibility to the materialistic thesis that the world of real existences is entirely material, and that nothing immaterial really exists, because we do not have senses for it.

The idea that the only thing that exists is matter, and that all things are composed of matter, and that everything is the mere result of material interactions makes Materialism not only very persuasive, but also very pervasive at the same

146

time: matter is the fundamental substance in nature. Consequently, *all* things, including mental aspects and consciousness, must be the result of material interactions, thus making mental and conscious processes merely by-products of material processes—that is, by-products of the biochemistry of the human brain and nervous system, for example. The physical world is literally *all* there is, says this mantra. Materialism emphatically proclaims that everything that exists is matter, and that matter is all there is.

Interestingly enough, Materialism also claims that "matter" is self-explanatory—it does not need any further explanation. Materialists may not explicitly express it that way, but for them matter is a "primary cause" (see Chapter 3) which needs no further explanation, and is responsible not only for things coming into existence, but also for their staying in existence, because nothing can exist, so they say, without the materials out of which it is made. The physicist Carl Sagan worded this view with great flair when he said that the material world is "all that is, or ever was, or ever will be."

What is wrong with Materialism?

If the doctrine of materialism were really true, then what are we to make of *thoughts*? How can thoughts be material? Of course, we can record our thoughts with a Dictaphone, which makes them material. And we can write our thoughts down on paper, which "materializes" them in another way. But what about the thoughts themselves? How can thoughts be material in and of themselves?

This momentous, skeptical question won't discourage materialists, though. They will quickly respond that thoughts are in fact material. Thoughts are, so they say, just a certain pattern of electrical impulses in the neurons of our brains.

But then, immediately, a serious problem arises. Unlike neurons, which do have material characteristics such as length, width, height, and weight, thoughts do not have any of those. Thoughts can be true or false, right or wrong, but never tall or short, heavy or light—they have no mass, no size, no color. We can think about sizes and colors of things, but the thoughts themselves do not have sizes and colors. Just as the brain cannot distinguish between legal and illegal narcotics, for example, so is the brain incapable of telling false thoughts apart from true beliefs—materially, they are identical, neurons firing. If I am certain that everything is physical, I would have no reason to suppose that this certainty is true—and hence I would have no reason to be certain that everything is physical, and physical only.

So as to evaluate the outcome of neural states as true or false, we need something that is *not* neural, for the simple reason that a pattern of electrical nerve impulses can't be true or false. As John C. Polkinghorne puts it, "neural events simply happen, and that is that." So there is no way to even think in terms of true or false, for as Stephen Barr notes, "One pattern of nerve impulses cannot be truer or less true than another pattern, any more than a toothache can be truer or less true than another toothache." Unlike brain processes, which are subject to physical causation, thoughts are subject to mental causation based on reason and intellect, on laws of logic and mathematics. The thought "one plus one," for instance, does not physically cause the answer "two." In other words, the brain does not secrete thoughts like the pancreas secretes hormones. Even brain scans can only pick up "brain waves," but never thoughts, for those fail to show up on pictures and scans, as they are immaterial.

There is something very peculiar about thoughts: They have *content*—they are *about* something, about something beyond themselves. But how could an assemblage of neurons—a group of material objects firing away—have any *content*? To use an analogy, anything that shows up on a computer monitor remains just an "empty" collection of "ones and zeros" that do not point beyond themselves until some kind of human interpretation gives sense and meaning to the display by interpreting it as being about something else. A thought may have a material substrate in a physical network such as the brain or a computer, but this material substrate only acts as a physical "carrier" for something immaterial—thoughts, that is—in the same way as newspapers carry thoughts of journalists. To think differently is like saying that Shakespeare's thoughts are nothing but ink marks on paper.

This outcome has serious consequences for Materialism itself. If materialists want to claim Materialism is true, then they should realize their very *thought* about Materialism must be more than a certain pattern of electrical activity in their brain cells. If thoughts were really material, based on neurons, impulses, and molecules, then they would be as fragile as the material they are supposedly based on. Besides, reducing thoughts to a "creation of neurons in the brain" obscures the fact that "neuron" itself is an abstract, immaterial concept in our thoughts. Such a claim starts a vicious circle. Stephen Barr shows us the vicious circle this way: "The very theory which says that theories are neurons firing is itself naught but neurons firing." If materialists want to claim Materialism is true, then they should realize this very thought must be more than a certain pattern of electrical activity in their brain cells, otherwise Materialism works like a boomerang that undermines its own foundation. In other words, Materialism is self-destructive. The statement that there are only material things is as fragile as the "material" that supposedly generated this world-view.

Thinking that Materialism is backed by science is another

misconception. Although many scientists are materialists, Materialism is not science, but merely a philosophical opinion. The most science can give us is the observation that many things in this Universe are material and can be quantified, measured, counted, and dissected. However, talking about "many things" does not entitle us to talk about "all things"—there is no way we could conclusively reason from "many" to "all." After having seen many white swans, for instance, one cannot safely conclude *all* swans are white. After having seen many material things, one cannot safely conclude that *all* things on earth are material—that conclusion is not logically justified. There is no way of knowing. One cannot even defend such arguments by saying they have worked so many times in the past, for that would be another example of moving from "many" to "all." This would take us on a never-ending search of proof.

Science on its own can never prove that matter is all there is, because science first limits itself exclusively to material things, and then says science shows us there is actually nothing but material things. It excludes immaterial entities ahead of time from our discourse, and then "concludes" there are only material entities. That is basically an example of circular reasoning: It begins with what it is trying to end with—that's how we keep circling around. If Materialism is true, we cannot even know that it is true. However, if matter were indeed all there is, then one should wonder what Materialism itself is. Another piece of matter? So there must be more than matter. This leaves definitely room for nonmaterial things such as logic, mathematics, philosophy, morality, and ultimately religious faith. Materialists, on the other hand, have a very limited outlook on things. If they come across phenomena that are hard to account for in terms of Materialism, they often end up by denying their very existence.

Ironically, in spite of all of the above, Materialism still has quite a "spiritual" appeal to it for some enigmatic reason. It allows for only one way of looking at the world. It is monopolistic by nature, and doesn't tolerate competitors. Instead, there should always be room for other views and perspectives on the world. Nothing entitles us to ignore that there is more to life than the material entities of molecules, neurons, and genes. The physician Tod Worner poses a serious question: "If matter is all there is, what is the mathematical constant pi?" If materialism is true, then immaterial entities such as pi cannot exist by themselves. And yet they do. In other words, there is so much in life that the thermometers and Geiger-tellers of Materialism can never capture—things such as thoughts, concepts, values, beliefs, laws, experiences, hopes, dreams, and ideals. There is no way Materialism can deal with these—other than denying them, but then it must deny itself as well.

So we must come to the conclusion that the doctrine of Materialism would at best be a dogmatic conviction, certainly not a scientific discovery or a conclusion of the empirical sciences. It is actually based on a circular argument: Materialism is true, because Materialism *must* be true. As Stephen Barr puts it, "Just as the astrologer believes that his life is controlled by the orbits of the planets, the materialist believes that his own actions and thoughts are controlled by the orbits of the electrons in his brain." It seems safe to say that Materialism is based on expectations and assumptions— certainly not proofs. In other words, it *assumes*, in advance, that nonmaterial objects cannot exist. But that assumption actually turns out to be self-destructive—it undermines its own nonmaterial assumption.

Gerard M. Verschuuren

Some side effects of Materialism

There is much more to Materialism—it has quite some repercussions. In treating matter as the only reality in the world, Materialism also denies the existence of God and the soul. Because of this implication, Materialism should be considered incompatible with most world religions. It actually puts matter in the position of God. That is not just a side-effect, of course, but in fact a very unnerving outcome.

But can Materialism really maintain the role of matter as an alternative to God who is considered the Primary Cause in religion? It is highly questionable whether this can be true. If matter is anything that has mass and takes up space, then it must be subject to motion and change. The Primary Cause, on the other hand, cannot be subject to motion and change, so we found out (see Chapter 2).

Besides, one could argue that matter cannot possibly be self-explanatory—it cannot explain its own existence. The idea that matter can cause itself and explain itself has rightly been caricaturized by Peter Kreeft as a magical "pop theory" that has things pop into existence without any cause. Nothing can just pop itself into existence; it must have a cause, because it does not and cannot have the power to make itself exist. For something to create itself, or produce itself, it would have to exist before it came into existence— which is logically and philosophically impossible. Causing its own existence is actually incoherent, because it presupposes its own existence.

Explaining matter in purely material terms is no explanation at all, but more like a circular argument. Saying that things are what they are and that they work the way they work is not a very satisfying explanation. Material things cannot account for their own existence for the simple reason that matter is that which by definition already exists. Yet, materialists seem to claim that matter is self-explanatory. They may not explicitly express it that way, but for them matter is a "primary cause" that needs no further explanation, and is responsible not only for things coming into existence, but for their staying in existence as well, because nothing can exist, so they say, without the materials out of which it is made. So they basically replace God as a primary cause with matter—which changes "matter" into "Matter" with a capital M. If materialists maintain that matter is in fact self-explanatory, uncaused, and necessary, then it would have distinctively "divine" qualifications, which would amount not to atheism but to pantheism—"god" being identical with the material world.

It is at this point that a serious question should arise: why is there something like matter rather than nothing? Those who say that there may be things that have no explanation should be told that we just provided an explanation in the previous paragraphs. Instead, they prefer to adopt something like a "black-box theory"—no more questions asked! But that theory is hard to accept, let alone to defend. If we say that nothing explains itself, and leave it at that, then we have come to the ir-rational conclusion that this Universe is absurd. If we follow instead a road to understanding, we can only restore rationality by stating that nothing explains itself, not even matter, and therefore needs an explanation "beyond" itself—God, the Primary Cause of all there is.

Michael Augros brings this argument to a close, "Matter itself is a product, receiving its very existence from the action of something before it." So God as the only Primary Cause, uncaused and motionless, remains standing; it is God who brings matter into existence and keeps it in existence. Matter cannot do so on its own. That's why matter cannot be a primary cause, regardless of how "fundamental" its role is in life. Nothing, not even matter, can just pop itself into existence; as we said earlier, it must have a cause, because it does not and cannot have the power to make itself exist. Besides, if matter were a first cause, it would be necessary instead of contingent. This would mean that everything about matter could be deduced by pure thinking without doing any observations or experiments—which is absurd too. Therefore, matter is contingent and needs an explanation beyond itself. It cannot explain its own existence, neither can it replace God.

If all of this regarding matter is true, then you may wonder why not the same could be said about God. In other words, what is it that caused the First Cause, or who created the Creator? The erroneous idea behind this question is that "everything needs a cause," but that statement would lead to an infinite regression. Instead we should rephrase the question as follows: "Everything that has come into existence needs a cause." Something that does not exist cannot bring itself into existence. But the Primary Cause never came into existence—which means God is the uncaused cause, the eternal cause who has always been in existence. Therefore, the question "Who created God?" is illogical, just like "To whom is a bachelor married?" is illogical. Secondary causes, which include matter, are contingent; that is to say, they don't have to exist, but because they do exist, we can ask for the cause of their existence. Matter does and can change, so there must be something that brings the change about. God, on the other hand, is a necessary, eternal, and unchanging being who did not come into existence but always has been, and therefore, doesn't need a cause to come into being.

Let's come to a more general conclusion. Matter may be everywhere, but it is certainly not all there is. If matter were indeed all there is, then one should wonder what Materialism itself is. If it's not another piece of matter, then there must be more than matter. This leaves definitely room for non-material things such as logic, mathematics, philosophy, rationality, morality, and ultimately religious faith. God is "the Creator of Heaven and Earth, of all that is seen and unseen," in the words of the Creed—that is, not only of all that is material but also of all that is immaterial, which includes the soul.

When materialists attack religion and declare it as nothing but a "deep-seated need to believe," in Carl Sagan's words, then they should at least realize that the same can be said about the defenders of Materialism—a "deep-seated need to believe." The Nobel Laureate and neurophysiologist John C. Eccles quite accurately described Materialism as "a religious belief held by dogmatic materialists... who often confuse their religion with their science."

Given all of the above, we must come to the conclusion that Materialism is a doctrine which is not only seriously flawed but also very destructive, even for itself.

11. Spiritism

What is Spiritism?

Most people take Spiritualism as a corrective to Materialism. Spiritualism is indeed a philosophical stance which holds, in general, that there is a spiritual realm of entities no less real than the material domain and, in particular, that the soul of man is a spiritual entity. As such, it is certainly not a destructive doctrine.

But this chapter is not about Spiritualism, it's about something else: Spiritism. The ideas of Spiritism can be traced back to Emanuel Swedenborg (1688-1772), a Swedish philosopher, seer, and theologian. In 1744, he claimed to have experienced visions of the spiritual world and talked with angels, devils, and spirits by visiting heaven and hell. Noticeable among later Spiritists was Andrew Jackson Davis, whose work, *The Principles of Nature* (1847), was dictated by him in trance. It contained a theory of the universe, closely resembling the Swedenborgian teachings.

The development of a more recent version of Spiritism dates from the year 1848 and from the experiences of the Fox sisters—Catherine, Leah, and Margaret—living in Rochester, New York. Strange "knockings" were heard in their house, pieces of furniture were moved about as though by invisible hands, and the noises became so troublesome that sleep was impossible. At length the "rapper" began to answer questions, and a code of signals was arranged to facilitate communication. It was also found that to receive messages special qualifications were needed. Since the Fox sisters had these, they are regarded as the first "mediums" of modern times.

In Europe, the way for Spiritism had been prepared by the Swedenborgian movement and by an epidemic of table-turning which spread from the Continent to England and invaded all classes of society. It was still a fashionable diversion when, in 1852, two mediums, Mrs. Hayden and Mrs. Roberts, came from America to London, and held séances which attracted wide attention.

A different branch of Spiritism, developed by Hippolyte Rivail under the pseudonym Allan Kardec, is today practiced mostly in Continental Europe and Latin America, especially in Brazil, and it emphasizes reincarnation. Kardec described his Spiritism as the study of "the nature, origin, and destiny of spirits, and their relation with the corporeal world." He reported observations of phenomena at séances that he attributed to incorporeal intelligence (spirits). He also spoke of "poltergeists," a type of ghost or spirit that is responsible for physical disturbances, such as loud noises and objects being moved or destroyed. He was eager, though, to distinguish Spiritism from Spiritualism.

Spiritism was also advocated by various periodical publications at the time, and defended in numerous works, some of which were said to have been dictated by the spirits themselves, e.g., the "Spirit Teachings" of Stainton Moses, which purport to give an account of conditions in the other world and form some sort of Spiritistic theology.

So, where does this hodgepodge of various beliefs and practices leave us? There seems to be a common core. Spiritism postulates that humans are essentially immortal spirits that temporarily inhabit physical bodies for several necessary incarnations to attain moral and intellectual improvement. It also asserts that spirits, through passive or active mediumship, may have beneficent or malevolent influence on the physical world. Consequently, Spiritism claims that it alone furnishes an incontestable proof of immortality, thus giving a death-blow to Materialism.

But its goals extend even further—namely, to establish a world-wide religion in which the adherents of the various traditional faiths, after setting their dogmas aside, can unite. If it has formulated no definite creed, and if its representatives differ in their attitudes toward the beliefs of Christianity, this is simply because Spiritism is expected to supply a new and fuller revelation which will either substantiate on a rational basis the essential Christian dogmas, or show that they are utterly unfounded. No wonder, Spiritism also has found earnest advocates among clergymen of various denominations, especially of the Universalist Unitarian Church. In short, it appealed strongly to many people who had lost all religious belief in a future life.

What is wrong with Spiritism?

It probably won't come as a surprise that the doctrine of Spiritism has met with much criticism and skepticism.

Not surprisingly, for those who deny the existence of a soul distinct from the organism—for instance, all who accept the fundamental ideas of Materialism (see Chapter 10)—it is a foregone conclusion that there can be no such communications as Spiritualism claims. But apart from any such a priori considerations, the opponents of Spiritism justify their skeptical position by pointing to innumerable cases of fraud which were brought to light either through the admissions of the mediums themselves or through closer examination of the methods they employed.

In 1851, the Fox girls were visited in Buffalo, NY by three physicians who were professors in the university of that city. As a result of their investigation, the doctors declared that the "raps" were simply "crackings" of the knee-joints. Then in 1853, the British physicist Michael Faraday, who became famous for his contributions to the study of electro-magnetism, showed that the table movements during séances were due to muscular action. Other factors of a physical nature have been mentioned—factors such as seismic activity or underground water movements. Psychological explanations have been suggested too: factors such as illusions, hallucinations, memory lapses, wishful thinking, or intentional deception. Other scientists came up with explanations for such phenomena that were based on hypnotism and telepathy. It was found that recourse to Spiritism frequently produces hallucinations and other aberrations, especially in subjects who have a mental weakness. They somehow trick themselves to enter into contact with their own subconscious. However, explanations like these did not lessen the popular enthusiasm about Spiritism.

But there may be an entirely different explanation—and arguably, the best explanation of them all: Spiritistic phenomena are caused by *demonic* intervention. For Catholics, the explanation of demonic intervention has special significance given the fact that the alleged communications with spirits are incompatible with the essential truths of religion, such as the Divinity of Christ, atonement and redemption, judgment and future retribution, while they encourage agnosticism, pantheism, and a belief in reincarnation.

The Catholic Church doesn't deny or reject that there may be ghosts. The Church has been contemplating, and trying to explain, ghostly manifestations for a long time. Much of that has been done through the uniquely Catholic concept of purgatory, where Peter Kreeft says many ghosts reside. Kreeft also says that there is "no contradiction" between ghosts and Catholic theology. "Ghosts appear on earth, but do not live on earth any longer," he says. "They are either in heaven, hell, or purgatory."

Yet, the Church denies or rejects Spiritism, its beliefs and its practices. According to the Catechism (2116),

> *All forms of divination are to be rejected: recourse to Satan or demons, conjuring up the dead or other practices falsely supposed to 'unveil' the future. Consulting horoscopes, astrology, palm readings, interpretation of omens and lots, the phenomena of clairvoyance, and recourse to mediums all conceal a desire for power over time, history, and, in the last analysis, other human beings, as well as a wish to conciliate hidden powers. They contradict the honor, respect, and loving fear that we owe to God alone.*

This analysis puts Spiritism in an entirely different context. The late Jesuit Father John Hardon explained that

> *behind the Church's attitude toward Spiritualism is the concern that a Catholic would expose himself to the risk of actually dealing with the evil spirit. The assumption is that if fraud or deception are excluded, and manifestations occur that are beyond natural explanation, the active agent in these cases is neither God nor any one of the good spirits (whether angelic or human) but demonic*

*forces that are sure to mislead the Catholic
and endanger the integrity of his faith.*

Catholic experts on the occult warn us that this widespread dabbling in the world of séances and psychics is anything but a harmless diversion. "Exact statistics are impossible to come by," said Father Lawrence Gesy, consultant on the occult for the Archdiocese of Baltimore. "But, as Jesus said, look around and see the signs of the times." As a matter of facts, turn on the TV and see the ads for psychic advisors, tarot card reading, psychic hotlines, books "channeled" through mediums, séances and every other type of occult activity are increasing. While the exact number of séances performed in America isn't available, a 1996 Gallup poll found that 20% of respondents think that such a thing might be possible.

Another American expert on the occult, Jesuit Father Mitchell Pacwa, says that the "old style" séances of the 19th century—gloomy parlors, levitating tables and so-called "spirit" rappings—have largely been replaced. "The old-style séances made popular by the Fox sisters in 1849 have given way to New Age 'channeling,'" he says. "In the old séances, the spirits would, supposedly, rap or tap out messages. These days, the medium goes into a trance and invites the spirit of the departed or the spirit of an advanced spiritual master or even the angels to speak through him or her."

Father Bamonte puts all of this in contrast to praying: "Every time we pray to God for our dead, without engaging in a spiritualistic practice, we ask the dead as well as the saints to pray to God with and for us." He calls this an in-vocation of the dead, but not their e-vocation, which is what Spiritism does. Then he adds, "The dead can only manifest themselves to us by the free initiative of God, directly and never through techniques or mediums such as spiritualistic séances. For serious reasons, God can allow a dead person to appear to us, for example, to give us advice or at least a consoling presence, to ask for prayers or to express gratitude for prayers offered."

Father Gesy, who has helped thousands of disillusioned occultists and New Agers during the last twenty-five years, warns us, "The [bereaved] person may be comforted at first, but those feelings fade. He may go back to the medium or perhaps become more deeply involved with the occult. We know that these spirits are not of God. God is not channeled. Nor are the saints, angels or souls of the deceased. For people who dabble in the occult, the end result is darkness, confusion and, often despair." Jesuit Father Philipp Schmidt gives us another good assessment of Spiritism when he writes, "where mirrors and windowpanes break in pieces ... where one can ring up on the telephone Napoleon, Cleopatra, Herod, or Paracelsus as though they were acquaintances from the rowing or the tennis club ... then spiritualistic nonsense begins."

How can Spiritism lure so many people? It shows how we have a restless desire to penetrate, by any and every means, the mystery that lies beyond death. While it is easy to condemn Spiritism as superstitious and vain, such a condemnation does not do away with the fact that Spiritism has become widespread in this age of destructive doctrines. How could this happen? G.K. Chesterton answered this question in his own idiosyncratic way: "[W]hen we cease to worship God, we do not worship nothing, we worship anything." Even the occult.

Some side effects of Spiritism

Ironically, Spiritism claims that spiritistic practices are real, but rejects at the same time the main reason why they could be real: satanic intervention. The problem of Spiritism is that it basically undermines the only, and arguably best, explanation for Spiritistic phenomena by denying the existence of Satan (see Chapter 3).

In response to this denial, the Catholic Church doesn't want us to forget that Satan is a real force to reckon with. If there is no Satan, then the Cross is a hoax; if there is no Satan, then the whole economy of salvation is up for grabs. No wonder Christianity sees the history of humanity as a perpetual, cosmic warfare between God and Lucifer, between good and evil, between the Light of God and the darkness of evil, between God calling us to be like His image and Satan enticing us to be our own image, which is Satan's image. Spiritism is another contender in this warfare.

It is not mere coincidence that Spiritism is connected with the *occult*. Interestingly enough, there are many links with the occult in the life of someone as evil as Adolf Hitler. His ideology of racial superiority and anti-Semitism was deeply intertwined with the occult "religion" of Madame Blavatsky, her so-called "Theosophy." She claimed to have received her occult doctrines during the seven years she spent in Tibet studying under Hindu masters. Her contempt for Jews and Judaism was undisguised. The swastika figured prominently in the seal of her society and was finally adopted as a dominant symbol by Hitler. Another link to the occult was Guido List who blended Theosophy with the occult use of the old Germanic runes and other occult practices, worshipping the Norse god Wotan. Early in his adult life, Hitler was a follower of List and probably even a formal member of his occult society.

A third link was Dietrich Eckart from another occult society. He predicted the imminent coming of a German messiah who would free Germany from the chains of Christianity. He also claimed to have "initiated" Hitler into occultism—a rite by which "higher centers" are opened, enabling extrasensory powers. In reality, it entails the introduction of demonic spirits into a person. On at least one occasion, Hitler referred to this man as his "John the Baptizer." And then there was at least a fourth link: Heinrich Himmler, who was never without his copy of the Hindu scriptures. He deeply believed in Eastern ideas such as reincarnation and karma. He established an institute in Berlin to study the potential of harnessing occult forces of power for the war effort, including black magic, spiritualist mediums, pendulum practitioners, and astrologers.

It is hard *not* to connect the occult and its practices with Satan. That's why Pope Benedict XVI would later write in his *Memoirs* that "Hitler was a demonic figure." Satan is definitely real! It is the power of Satan that enabled evil men such as Hitler, Stalin, Mao, Pol Pot, and Osama bin Laden to spellbind and enslave the minds and spirits of millions, creating hell ahead of time, right here on earth. Who else could have given such people their superhuman power? In fact, they sold their souls by following "orders" that stem from sources far beyond their own resources. Some satanic force, engaged in a battle against God's creation, gave these people more than mere human power. The Catechism (2851) makes it very clear, "[E]vil is not an abstraction, but refers to a person, Satan, the Evil One, the angel who opposes God." It is God's aim for each one of us to attain Heaven after death, whereas Satan's aim is to ensure that as many people as possible miss that eternal goal.

Not only does this cosmic warfare occur on the large scale of history, it also rages on the small scale of each person's inner self. That's where decisions are being made either *for* or *against* God. Satan works day and night on the personal battlefield of our souls—even through the use of black magic, mediums, spirit rappings, clairvoyants, séances, tarot card readings, and palm readings. The occult is one of Satan's favorite weapons. The fuel behind dabbling in the occult is some satanic force engaged in a battle against God's creation—which is the role of Satan, the "father" of all lies, the great divider who knows how to remain hidden behind the scene.

Satan is happy to lend us some "spiritual" help to do whatever is against God's commandments. It is Satan's ultimate goal to demolish all Christian elements in society and to damage the human image, which was made in the image of God. Satan is in constant communication with our souls, if we let him. Letting him in is even more dangerous when we are unaware of the battle that is taking place in our souls. That's why Satan loves to hide or disguise himself. To deny he even exists is one of Satan's best ploys.

Let's make clear, though, that Satan is not the opposite of God. He is not some kind of anti-god. According to the Bible, Satan is a created being, originally created by God as His most powerful angelic helper (see Chapter 3). But God gave his angels freedom as much as he gave us freedom to turn either for or against God. So, Satan is merely a creature, an angel who rebelled against God. Ever since, he continues to prowl the earth like a ravenous, roaring lion "looking for someone to devour" (2 Pet. 5:8). Satan and the other evil spirits prowl about the world for the ruin of souls. No wonder they feel at home in the occult.

Archbishop Fulton Sheen provided us with a keen insight into Satan:

> Do not mock the Gospels and say there is no Satan. Evil is too real in the world to say that. Do not say the idea of Satan is dead and gone. Satan never gains so many cohorts, as when, in his shrewdness, he spreads the rumor

that he is long since dead. Do not reject the Gospel because it says the Savior was tempted. Satan always tempts the pure—the others are already his.

Given all of the above, we must come to the conclusion that Spiritism is a doctrine which is not only seriously flawed but also very destructive.

12. Scientism

What is Scientism?

Undoubtedly, science has one of the most impressive track records in human history. It is a success story that keeps persistently adding new achievements, with no end in sight. So it shouldn't come as a surprise that science has given us reason, not only for high hopes, but also for extravagant claims. Its success was made possible because it focuses its research on *matter*, which can be dissected, counted, quantified, and measured (see Chapter 10). Based on this connection with matter, the following conclusion seems to be warranted for many supporters of science: if there is only material stuff in the Universe, and if science deals exclusively with "matter," science must be the ideal method to study the Universe.

This ongoing success story has made us believe there is no corner of the Universe, no dimension of reality, no feature of human existence beyond what science can reach. In other words, all our questions deserve, and actually must have, a scientific answer phrased in terms of particles, quantities, and equations—and if not yet, we must work on finding that scientific answer. From now on, "the real world" is considered to be a world of quantifiable, material entities.

The basic idea behind this is that the scientific method is not only the best method there is, but also the only method we have to understand the world. This idea has become a doctrine and is called "Scientism." The dogma of Scientism is that science is the one and only method to give us reliable knowledge about ourselves and the world around us. It portrays scientists as a bunch of white-coated people—emotion-free and assumption-free—who battle collectively to wrest secrets from the stubborn Universe. Scientism has a dogmatic, rigid belief in the omni-competence of science. Its claim is that there is no other point of view than the "scientific" world-view. Thus we end up with an unshakable conviction about what counts as knowledge—and a very restrictive one at that.

As the biologist E. O. Wilson puts it, "Science for its part will test relentlessly every assumption about the human condition." The physicist Carl Sagan agrees with him: "I don't want to believe. I want to know." The chemist Peter Atkins claims something similar: "Religion, in contrast to science, deploys the repugnant view that the world is too big for our understanding." And rather recently the biologist Richard Dawkins joined the choir, "There's no point of having faith if you have evidence." He also speaks of "claims about the world that on analysis turn out to be scientific claims."

What this boils down to is that there are no truths other than scientific truths—that is, truths that have been corroborated, or at least can potentially be corroborated, by using scientific tools and scientific methods. Truths that do not meet this condition are not really truths but at best illusions or make-believe opinions. Reliable knowledge can only be gained through rigorous scientific testing. All the rest is of highly dubious quality and therefore not worth serious consideration. In brief, what can't be counted doesn't count.

Based on this doctrine, some scientists, especially with many Nobel Laureates among them, think that their authority and expertise in a tiny segment of science entitles them to proclaim authoritative statements about everything else outside that small segment. They use their scientific expertise to make us think they must be experts in everything else as well. Some of them use their scientific authority to churn out, with the speed of light, books that promote opinions and views that go far beyond their field of expertise. This easily takes them into philosophical and metaphysical debates—often without them even realizing it— because Scientism tells them their scientific expertise is adequate anywhere in the Universe. It is Scientism that makes them believe their scientific expertise is proficient for any area of human interest. So they can use the technique of raising question-begging philosophical objections disguised as scientific objections.

Scientists fascinated by the doctrine of Scientism also think they are free from any extra-scientific influences. They assume there is nothing more to material reality than what science tells us. They proclaim themselves "free" of any world-view, any viewpoints, any philosophy, or any values. They believe that there is no worldview and no metaphysics in what they claim. If there is any "metaphysics" in their claims, it is a meta-physics "reduced" to physics. All scientific truths are supposed to be "pure" and "naked" truths that only science has access to.

What is wrong with Scientism?

Scientism sounds so simple and unbeatable that many just swallow it. However, Scientism deserves some serious scrutiny. Let's start with a very simple objection—problem #1. Those who defend scientism seem to be unaware of the fact that Scientism itself does not follow its own rule. How could science ever prove all by itself that science is the only way of finding truth? There is no experiment that could do the trick. We cannot test Scientism in the laboratory or with a double-blind experiment. Science on its own cannot answer questions that are beyond the reach of its empirical and experimental techniques.

Scientism claims that a method as successful as the one that science provides would disqualify any other methods—problem #2. This is obviously an assumption, not a conclusion. A blood test, for instance, is an excellent method to assess a person's health. But there are many other reliable methods, such as X-rays, MRIs, etc., depending on what we are trying to assess. But a blood test on its own cannot be used to prove that a blood test is the best, let alone only, method there is. Yet, that's what Scientism does: First it declares science's empirical and experimental techniques as far superior to other methods, and then claims that this disqualifies any other methods. The fact that a metal detector, for instance, is a perfect tool to detect metals does not make it a perfect tool for detecting anything else. As Edward Feser puts it, "That a method is especially useful for certain purposes simply does not entail that there are no other purposes worth pursuing nor other methods more suitable to those other purposes."

One cannot talk about science the way Scientism does without stepping outside science—problem #3. A statement *about* science can only be made from *outside* science. When scientism declares there is nothing outside the domain of science, it must be making a statement from outside the domain of science, which cannot be tested with tools and methods from inside the domain of science. Science cannot pull itself up by its own bootstraps—any more than an electric generator is able to run on its own power.

Claiming that nothing can be true unless it can be proven scientifically cannot itself be proven scientifically—problem #4. This claim is not a scientific discovery but at best a philosophical or metaphysical assumption from outside the domain of science—and a poor one at that. It declares everything outside science as a despicable form of metaphysics, in defiance of the fact that all those who reject metaphysics are in fact committing their own version of metaphysics. This makes Scientism a totalitarian ideology, for it allows no room for anything but itself. Such a mistake makes for megalomania: science becomes a know-all and cure-all, without any further validation.

Scientism focuses exclusively on what can be scientifically tested, and then rejects anything that cannot be scientifically tested—problem #5. *Neglecting* what is outside the scope of science may be a wise scientific strategy, but *rejecting* what is outside its scope goes one step further and turns inevitably into a baseless, unjustifiable ideology. Indeed, science has a rather narrow scope restricted to what can be measured, dissected, counted, and quantified. But therein also lies its limitation. First it limits itself exclusively to what can be measured, dissected, counted, and quantified, and then declares anything else as nonexistent because it cannot be measured, dissected, counted, and quantified. That is a form of circular reasoning. A sign hung in Albert Einstein's office at Princeton University advised us differently: "Not everything that can be counted counts; not everything that counts can be counted." The Austrian physicist and Nobel Laureate Erwin Schrödinger once said about science, "It knows nothing of beautiful and ugly, good or bad, God and eternity."

Scientism basically dismisses anything that cannot be tested and corroborated by science—problem #6. In doing so it rejects what it neglects. Interestingly enough, the astonishing successes of science have not been gained by answering every kind of question, but precisely by refusing to do so. We shouldn't forget that science has purchased success at the cost of limiting its ambition—therefore, it can't claim *universal* validity for its *local* successes. Whatever we neglect we cannot automatically reject. Everything that cannot be dissected, measured, counted, or quantified is off-limits for science. Science should never forget that it is "blind" for many aspects of life that are not material, and therefore off-limits. So saying that those aspects are not worth knowing is as fallacious, in the words of Feser, as claiming in college that "the fact that you have only taken courses you knew you would excel in shows that the other classes aren't worth taking."

The success of the scientific method does not make it an omnipotent tool—problem #7. The success of metal detectors, as said earlier, gives us no reason to conclude that there are no nonmetallic features of reality. Neither can a thermometer tell us that temperature is all there is; it can only successfully measure what exactly the temperature is. In other words, science can only tell us something about one aspect of the world: its scientific aspect. But that doesn't preclude other aspects and views. That's why the late University of California at Berkeley philosopher of science Paul Feyerabend, for instance, could say, "[S]cience should be taught as one view among many and not as the one and only road to truth and reality." Even the "positivistic" philosopher Gilbert Ryle expressed a similar view: "[T]he nuclear physicist, the theologian, the historian, the lyric poet and the man in the street produce very different, yet compatible and even complementary pictures of one and the same 'world.'" Science provides only one of these views.

How can scientism claim that scientific knowledge is a superior form of knowledge—problem #8? True, it may be more easily testable than other kinds, but it is also very restricted and therefore requires additional forms of knowledge. Even if we were to agree that the scientific method gives us better testable results than many other sources of knowledge, this would still not entitle us to claim that only the scientific method gives us genuine knowledge of reality. As we said earlier, a metal detector is a perfect tool to locate metals, but that does not mean a metal detector is a tool superior to any other tools. There is no way metal detectors can tell us anything about the existence of stones or plants. An instrument can only detect what it is designed to detect.

Scientism lets its favorite technique dictate what is considered "real" in life—problem 9#. To best characterize this restricted attitude of Scientism, an image used by the late psychologist Abraham Maslow might be helpful: If you only have a hammer, every problem begins to look like a nail. So instead of idolizing our "scientific hammer," we should acknowledge that not everything is a "nail." No wonder this has led some to criticize scientism as a form of circular reasoning. The late philosopher Ralph Barton Perry expressed this as follows: "A certain type of method is accredited by its applicability to a certain type of fact; and this type of fact, in turn, is accredited by its lending itself to a certain type of method." That's how we keep circling around. Instead, we should let reality determine which techniques are appropriate for which parts of reality, and not reversed.

Scientism asserts that science is about material things only—problem 10#. Nonetheless, scientific research requires immaterial things such as logic and mathematics. Logic and mathematics are not physical, and therefore not testable by the natural sciences—and yet they cannot be ignored or denied by science. In fact, science heavily relies on logic and mathematics to interpret the data that scientific observation and experimentation provide. Yet, these immaterial things are real and indispensable, even though they are beyond scientific observation. Take, for instance, the mathematical concept of "pi" (π). As the particle physicist Stephen Barr points out, this concept is not some private experience, like a toothache; it is not a material object like a melon; it is more than a sensation or a neurological artifact; it is certainly more than a certain pattern of neurons firing in the brain; it is not even a property of material things, for there are no pi-sided melons—perhaps close, but never exactly. Instead, "pi" is a precise and definite concept with logical relationships to other equally precise concepts. No material thing has the perfection that geometrical objects have, so these truths do not depend on the material world.

Ironically, Scientism itself is one of those immaterial things it rejects—problem 11#. It exclusively dedicates itself to what is material and can be dissected, counted, measured, and quantified. But then Scientism kicks in and says that there is nothing else in this world than that which is material and can be dissected, measured, counted, or quantified. However, this verdict itself is not material and cannot be dissected, counted, measured, or quantified. An immaterial claim like this acts like a boomerang that comes back to hit whoever launched it.

Scientism's favorite science is physics, because all other sciences should, and will in time, be reduced to physics, so it claims—problem #12. However, not any kind of science, not even physics, is able to declare itself a superior form of knowledge. Some scientists have argued, for example, that physics always has the last word in observation, for the observers themselves are physical. But why not say then that psychology always has the last word, because these observers are interesting psychological objects as well? Neither statement makes sense; observers are neither physical nor psychological, but they can indeed be studied from a physical, biological, psychological, or statistical viewpoint—which is an entirely different matter.

Science can never cover "all there is" the way scientism

claims—problem #13. True, there may someday be a "Grand Unified Theory" (GUT) in physics—a theory that unifies the three non-gravitational forces (the electromagnetic force, the weak nuclear force, and the strong nuclear force)—but that is not the same as a "Grand Unified Theory of *Everything*." A theory of "all there is" would have to explain also why some people believe in it and some do not. Limiting oneself exclusively to a particular perspective such as physics is in itself at best a metaphysical decision. One cannot give science the metaphysical power it does not possess.

Science can never claim ultimate authority, as Scientism would like to have it—problem #14. Scientism causes scientists to easily forget that they went through hyper-specialized training in a narrow field of science coupled with a lack of exposure to other disciplines and methods. If they claim expertise in everything else as well, they are like plumbers trying to also fix our electricity at home—or like electricians attempting to fix our plumbing. What gets lost in the process is the awareness that expertise in one field may not help much in handling problems of another field. This also may obscure the fact that scientists nowadays are highly specialized. One could even agree with the late Nobel Laureate and biologist Konrad Lorenz that a scientist "knows more and more about less and less and finally knows everything about nothing."

Science lives by the grace of certain assumptions, which Scientism denies—problem #15. Edward Feser convincingly argues that scientists must assume that there is an objective world external to their minds. They must assume that this world is governed by regularities captured in scientific laws. They must assume that their methodology can uncover and accurately describe these regularities; and so forth. Since their scientific methodology presupposes these things, it cannot attempt to justify them without arguing in a circle. To break out of this circle requires taking the position of an extra-scientific vantage point which pretends that science conveys an accurate picture of reality—and, if Scientism is to be justified, that only science, and science alone, does so. As Feser concludes, "But then the very existence of that extrascientific vantage point would falsify the claim that science *alone* gives us a rational means of investigating objective reality."

In spite of all the above objections, Scientism is still very much alive, albeit mostly unspoken or even hidden underground. The late Dutch physicist Hendrik Casimir—the Casimir effect of quantum-mechanical attraction was named after him—once said, "We have made science our God." Indeed, scientism has become a "semi-religion" of which the scientists are considered the "priests." Science is supposed to explain everything, but then in a much better way than God once did according to this view. It is in this frame of mind that the late Stephen Hawking once exclaimed, "[O]ur goal is a complete understanding of the events around us and of our own existence." Yes, you read it right: even a *complete* understanding of our own existence. Well, science may be everywhere, but science is certainly not all there is—claiming differently would amount to a flawed and destructive doctrine. In our schools, we should teach science, not preach it!

Some side effects of Scientism

Scientism has been a doctrine so powerful that it has gone as far as infiltrating the thoughts of certain people about religion and theology as well. Someone like the nearly legendary Jesuit Fr. Teilhard de Chardin, for instance, was so impressed by science that he and others decided to mix science and religion together into one single concoction.

People like him tend to speak in terms of "reconciliation," as if science and religion were just two different ways of expressing the same truth, thus ignoring that science has its own truths, as does religion. Yet, promoters of "reconciliation" want to fuse two different perspectives into one. This can go into two opposite directions: either science annexes religion or religion takes over science. However, if you mix them together, you are basically trying to mix water and oil.

The most common outcome of a fusion between science and religion is that science monopolizes religion—by "interpreting" the data of religion, that is—so as to leave the data of science intact. The common reason given for this is that scientific facts are considered to be "safe" and "proven," whereas religious facts are seen as dubious. Obviously, we have another case here of Scientism. Hence, new scientific developments are supposed to lead to a revamping of religious doctrine, for science trumps everything else in this view.

However, we should question why religion should bend to the criteria of science. Science cannot claim such authority, as we discussed extensively in the previous chapter. Another reason is that what we call "proven" scientific knowledge is only proven until a new set of empirical data "disproves" what was previously considered "proven." In science, whatever is true today may not be true tomorrow. Science is always a work in progress. Francis Crick, one of the two scientists who discovered DNA, couldn't have said it better: "A theory that fits all the facts is bound to be wrong, as some of the facts will be wrong." Crick could have said this more accurately; facts cannot be wrong, but what we thought were facts turned out *not* to be facts.

This happens much more than you might think. There are many scientific theories that were believed to be true but sooner or later turned out to be false. Here is just a small selection of such cases. (1) Vulcan was a planet that nineteenth century scientists believed to exist somewhere between Mercury and the Sun in order to explain certain peculiarities about Mercury's orbit. (2) The expanding Earth hypothesis stated that phenomena like underwater mountain ranges and continental drift could be explained by the fact that our planet was gradually growing larger. (3) Prior to scientists embracing the notion that the Universe was created as the result of the Big Bang, it was commonly believed that the size of the Universe was an unchanging constant. (4) As peptic ulcers became more common in the 20th century, doctors increasingly linked them to the stress of modern life, until the Australian clinical researcher Barry Marshal discovered that the bacterium *Helicobacter pylori* caused peptic ulcer disease. (5) For some 30 years, the number of human chromosomes was supposed to be 48, until the geneticist Joe Tjio found it to be 46 in 1955. And there are many more examples of revised scientific theories.

The second possible outcome of a fusion between science and religion is that religion conquers and suppresses science by transforming scientific data into a religious amalgam. But such a route is dangerous as well; it has been tried out many times—most recently by proponents of creationism— declaring "the Bible is right and science is wrong"—or by fans of the "intelligent design theory," who claim that scientific processes in evolution sometimes need periodic divine interventions. Here we have another attempt to create a mixture of "oil and water." But again, these two just do not mix well together, for religion is very different from science, with each having its own kind of truths. What is true of Catholic doctrine today will also be true tomorrow. But not so in science: what is true today may have to be revised tomorrow based on new and better experiments and theories. In other words, scientists must submit their minds to the data of experiment, religious believers must submit theirs to the data of Revelation.

The contrast we painted here may raise some questions. It is easy to see that what is true today in science may have to be revised tomorrow. But would this not also be true of Catholic doctrine? The answer depends on what Revelation means and what it tells us. Divine Revelation is always progressive in nature—that is, over time, we are granted a fuller and fuller knowledge of God in general, including a fuller understanding of the meaning of prior Revelation. For instance, the New Testament does not abolish the truth of the Old Testament but extends and deepens it. Although Revelation came to its fullest manifestation in Jesus, its understanding would still need further completion. Many of the central doctrines of Christianity, including the Trinitarian nature of God, the divinity of Jesus, the resurrection of Jesus from the dead, and the perpetual virginity of Mary, only gradually became clear in the centuries following Jesus' death. Our understanding of divine truth became better and clearer—although we may never reach a full understanding in this life. This process of growth resembles the way a river growths—it gets wider and deeper, while remaining the same river.

During this continuing process, some truths were proclaimed by the Church as divinely revealed, so they became dogmas, to distinguish them from more optional interpretations. Dogmas must be held by all as essential for Catholic faith. Hence, the Church cannot deny in one age what she has affirmed in a previous age as essential dogma. True, the Church did change her interpretation of the Bible every once in a while, but such interpretations are not unchanging dogmas; they were never proclaimed as divinely revealed. Obviously, geocentrism has never been declared a dogma, and evolution will never be declared a dogma. Our salvation does not depend on whether we believe in heliocentrism, evolution, or any other scientific theory.

The bottom line of this discussion is that scientists must submit their minds to the data of experiment, while religious believers must submit theirs to the data of Revelation. In other words, do not mix them together but respect their different authorities and their different kinds of truths. Science requires a questioning attitude, whereas Catholicism is based on an affirming attitude. They both have their own autonomous domain. It is in their respective domains that science and religion function best. So there is good reason to keep them separated. Keeping them distinguished prevents trespassing attempts and border conflicts, for good fences make good neighbors. Science should not invade the domain of religious issues, and religion should not intrude into the domain of scientific issues. Science and religion are not competitors; they are neighbors, each one with their own domain, perspective, and authority.

If we do not honor the separation between science and religion, science may become a pseudo-religion, and religion may become a semi-science. Instead, we should keep them separate. On the one hand, science could never silence religion, for there's no scientific proof that science is the only way to gain truth. On the other hand, religion could never silence science, for there is no religious proof that religion is the only way to gain truth. Neither one can claim exclusivity, but together they make for a more comprehensive outlook on life.

Regardless of what we said so far about their differences, there is still a deep, hidden-away connection between science and religion. This statement may look very strange and enigmatic at first sight, so let me explain what this "mysterious" connection is.

Two important pillars science is based on are the

following two assumptions: the world is *orderly* and the world is *intelligible*. Let's discuss them separately, beginning with the assumption that the world is orderly. This assumption is not as evident as you might think. In utter amazement, Albert Einstein wrote in one of his letters, "But surely, a priori, one should expect the world to be chaotic, not to be grasped by thought in any way." And yet, the world is not chaotic but orderly. As Dimitri Mendeleev, who discovered the Periodic Table of Elements, put it, "It is the function of science to discover the existence of a general reign of order in nature and to find the causes governing this order."

Where does the order of the world come from? The notion of order certainly does not come from science itself. Science on its own can never prove there is order in this world, but instead must assume it. Scientists must assume that the world has an orderly structure—otherwise there would be no reason for them to pursue science. So order is definitely not the outcome of intense and extensive scientific research. The powerful tool of falsification, for instance, is in fact based on this very assumption: the fact that scientific evidence can refute a scientific hypothesis is only possible if there is indeed order in this Universe. Without order, there could not be any falsifying evidence—it would just be a disorderly exception. When we do find falsifying evidence, we don't take this as proof that the Universe is not orderly, but as an indication that there is something wrong with the specific order we had conjectured up in our minds. Counter-evidence does allow us to falsify theories, but never the principle of falsification itself.

In other words, order in the Universe is not a scientific discovery but a proto-scientific assumption that makes science possible. Order is a proto-scientific notion that must come first before science can even get off the ground. It is one of the main pillars of science.

This tells us that order must come from somewhere else. If it were merely an assumption, the idea of order in the universe might turn out to be an illusion. However, the assumption works! How come? The best, and probably only, explanation is that the existence of an "orderly" Creator explains why there is order in this world. The Book of Wisdom (11:20) says about the order God created, "You have arranged all things by measure and number and weight." Hence the only way to find out what this order looks like and what the Creator has actually done is to go out, look, and measure—which opens the door for scientific exploration. The only way to find out is to "interrogate" the Universe by investigation, exploration, and experiment. It is through scientific experiments that we can "read" God's mind, so to speak.

Something similar could be said about the other assumption, the other pillar of science: the world is intelligible and comprehensible. This assumption is not evident either. Albert Einstein worded it well, "The most incomprehensible thing about the universe is that it is comprehensible." And yet, scientists must assume that the world is comprehensible and intelligible—otherwise there would be no reason for them to pursue science. Science cannot prove this, for if something in science is still incomprehensible, scientists keep searching until it does become comprehensible. In other words, the intelligibility of the Universe is not a scientific discovery but a proto-scientific assumption that makes science possible. Order is a proto-scientific notion that must come first before science can even begin. It is another main pillar of science.

This strongly suggests that the intelligibility of the world must also come from somewhere else. Again, if it were just an assumption, that could be a deceiving guess. Instead, the assumption works! The physical order we observe in this world appears to be amazingly "consistent." It is a consistency that must perplex us, for how is it possible that reality can be "grasped" by reason? Yet, not only is our rationality consistent, but so is the world itself. The "mystery" we have here is the fact that the rationality present in our minds matches the rationality we find in the world. The conformity and harmony between the divine rationality in Creation and the human rationality found in the human mind must be a riddle for non-believers, but for religious believers it would be "a match made in Heaven."

In the Catholic view, only God is the source where the order and intelligibility of the Universe ultimately stem from. The Universe is the orderly creation of a rational Intellect capable of being rationally interrogated. Only God's rationality can explain that the world is an objective and orderly entity accessible though the human mind because the mind too is an orderly and objective product of the same rational and consistent Creator. Fr. George Lemaître, who launched the Big Bang theory, once spoke about the God of the Big Bang as the "One Who gave us the mind to understand him and to recognize a glimpse of his glory in our Universe which he has so wonderfully adjusted to the mental power with which he has endowed us."

Even scientists, or especially scientists, must be baffled by all of this. Even if they are devoted to the doctrine of Scientism, they cannot but uphold the conviction that there is an intelligible plan behind this Universe, a plan that is accessible to the human intellect through the natural light of reason. No wonder Albert Einstein was very definite on this. He had to acknowledge, "Everyone who is seriously involved in the pursuit of science becomes convinced that a Spirit is manifest in the laws of the Universe—a Spirit vastly superior to that of man." He also expressed very emphatically his "confidence in the rational nature of reality and in its being accessible, to some degree, to human reason. When this feeling is missing, science degenerates into mindless empiricism." And Einstein was certainly not alone on this. The late astrophysicist Sir James Jeans would put it this way, "[T]he Universe begins to look more like a great thought than a great machine." And the physicist Paul Davies said at one point, "There must be an unchanging rational ground in which the logical, orderly nature of the universe is rooted." Many other scientists would agree, albeit often silently.

So we must come to a rather perplexing conclusion: we actually need religion to explain why reason as used in science does in fact work. Only belief in a Creator God can explain why there is an almost perfect harmony between the rationality of our minds and the rationality found in the world around us. It's this very Judeo-Christian concept of a Creator God that makes science possible. Only God can be the ultimate source where the order as well as the intelligibility of the Universe ultimately stem from. Thanks to the rationality of human beings, made in the image of God, we can see the world as being orderly and comprehendsible. Without the religious idea that the Universe is a rational and intelligent creation endowed with order and intelligibility, science would most likely not be possible and would most likely never have emerged. One could even make the case that denying or neglecting the existence of God would eat away the very foundation of science. This is definitely another nail on the coffin of Scientism.

Given all of the above, we must come to the conclusion that scientism is a doctrine which is not only seriously flawed but also very destructive.

13. Transhumanism

What is Transhumanism?

As the term indicates, Transhumanism is a take-off of Humanism (see Chapter 5). Transhumanism—sometimes abbreviated as H+ or h+—is an intellectual movement that aims to transform the human condition by developing sophisticated technologies and making them widely available to greatly enhance human intellect and physiology. It is in essence a belief in the perfectibility of human beings, with the aspiration of enhancing, and even transcending, the capacities of the human being.

The most common transhumanist thesis is that human beings may eventually be able to transform themselves into different beings with abilities so greatly expanded from the current condition as to merit the label of "post-human beings." Transhumanism wishes to surpass what we think is humanly possible. What Transhumanism strives for is not just the betterment of the human condition, but the creation of something better than the human condition as we know it. In other words, whatever the human being and its human capacities may be, technology can transcend them.

Transhumanism has not a long history. More specific ideas of transhumanism were first advanced in 1923 by the British geneticist J. B. S. Haldane in his essay *Daedalus: Science and the Future*, which predicted that great benefits would come from applications of advanced sciences to human biology. But more precisely, the biologist Julian Huxley is often regarded as the founder of Transhumanism. In 1951, Huxley gave a lecture that proposed a non-religious version of the ideas of Fr. Teilhard de Chardin. "Such a broad philosophy," he wrote, "might perhaps be called, not Humanism, because that has certain unsatisfactory connotations, but Transhumanism. It is the idea of humanity attempting to overcome its limitations and to arrive at fuller fruition."

What all supporters of the doctrine of Transhumanism have in common is their belief that humans can and should use new technologies to become *more* than human. This way, it has developed into some form of "techno-utopianism," focused on the role of technology in creating a new world. It envisions a technological utopia. In general, Technological Utopianism views technology's developments and impacts as extremely positive.

The transhumanist Ray Kurzweil, who was given in 2012 a director of engineering position at Google, wrote in 2006, "The human species, along with the computational technology it created, will be able to solve age-old problems... and will be in a position to change the nature of mortality in a postbiological future." Soon we could reach the point at which we would be transformed into what Kurzweil called "Spiritual Machines." We would transfer or "resurrect" our minds onto supercomputers, allowing us to live forever. Our bodies would become incorruptible, immune to disease and decay, and we would acquire knowledge by uploading it to our brains. This is humanism stretched to its extreme.

This thought started a new trend of freezing parts of the body, waiting for these anticipated transhumanist developments to materialize. Being frozen, in anticipation of developments, is rather expensive. It would cost you $80,000 for just the head, which is the most popular option, and

$200,000 for the whole body. Those who sign up for this post-death procedure do so in the hope that by the time they are unfrozen there will be a transhumanist cure for death. The preferred scenario probably is that you upload the brain into a new body, and the old fleshy body is disposed of.

Believe it or not, but Transhumanists today wield enormous power in Silicon Valley—entrepreneurs such as Elon Musk and Peter Thiel identify themselves as believers— where they have founded think-tanks such as the Singularity University and the Future of Humanity Institute. The ideas proposed by the pioneers of the movement are no longer abstract theoretical musings but are being embedded into emerging technologies at organizations such as Google, Apple, Tesla and SpaceX.

The most extreme representative of Transhumanism, of more in particular Techno-Utopianism, is probably the British cryptologist I. J. Good. He wrote already in 1965:

> *Let an ultraintelligent machine be defined as a machine that can far surpass all the intellectual activities of any man however clever. Since the design of machines is one of these intellectual activities, an ultraintelligent machine could design even better machines; there would then unquestionably be an "intelligence explosion," and the intelligence of man would be left far behind. Thus the first ultraintelligent machine is the last invention that man need ever make.*

What is wrong with Transhumanism?

The ideas of Transhumanism have been launched before. The Industrial Revolution fostered the expectation that technology was going to solve the world's and man's problems. It did not happen, of course; it just created a world of machines, without improving other aspects of human life such as happiness, prosperity, health, sexuality, suffering, morality, and the like. It was an illusion then, so why not now?

For many, the utopia of a society that adopts human enhancement technologies has come to resemble the dystopia depicted in the 1932 novel *Brave New World*, by Aldous Huxley. Instead of humanizing society, it may be experienced as de-humanizing society. In his 1958 book *Brave New World Revisited*, written also by Huxley, he concluded that the world was indeed becoming like *Brave New World*—but much faster than he originally thought. As G. K. Chesterton explained, Huxley was revolting against the "Age of Utopias," against the idea that humanity would solve all economic and social issues.

Like with all utopias, Transhumanism paints a rather rosy picture of new scientific and technological advances. This picture can easily obscure that there are serious downsides to these advances. Although more and more people seem to bow down in adoration before the altar of Transhumanism, it is an altar on which many victims have been sacrificed. Just think of the horrors of the 20th century such as two world wars, a Cold War, and three totalitarian regimes with death camps—plus the horrors of the 21st century such as nuclear proliferation and terrorism with its suicide bombers. These developments should caution us for extravagant optimism. Evil is seen as a merely technological problem—not as a problem that permeates human life.

But the criticism doesn't end here. Transhumanism promises us things that it hasn't been able to fulfill so far, and arguably may never be able to fulfil. Their promises run widely, from an indefinite extension of life to a definite abolition of suffering. They love to speak and think in "super" terms: "super-longevity," "super-intelligence," and "super well-being." However, when speaking of the promise of "super well-being," the Transhumanist vision assumes a very narrow understanding of happiness, equating it with the absence of suffering. Their favorite expression is "phasing out suffering." C.S. Lewis anticipated this and labeled it the "abolition of man." The abolition of man would come about when science and technology found that the last frontier in the conquest of nature was humanity itself. "Human nature will be the last part of Nature to surrender to Man," Lewis warned.

Another problem of Transhumanism is that it is strongly rooted in Scientism (see Chapter 12), including all the flaws that come with that doctrine. It equates scientific progress to progress in social, humanitarian, moral, and religious areas, which is basically a form of scientism. It is easy to see that scientific progress does not automatically lead to progress in other areas of human interest, because science is not omnipotent; it's not a know-all, nor a cure-all. History is our witness.

Not only is Transhumanism rooted in Scientism, it also has a strong gnostic overtone (see Chapter 3). It has a palpable contempt for humanity in its actual state, and the contempt is above all directed at the human body. Referring to the human body scornfully as a "meat sack" or "meat bag" is a common term among many transhumanists. They expect technology to liberate us from the confines of human flesh. This is the latest gnostic way of liberating us from the dungeon of the human body. The British moral philosopher Mary Midgley characterizes the ideas of Transhumanism as "quasi-scientific dreams and prophesies" involving visions of escape from the body coupled with "self-indulgent, uncontrolled power-fantasies"—perhaps even similar to the

Gerard M. Verschuuren

secret knowledge Gnosticism claim. This time it's the elite of Silicon Valley that have been enlightened with the right knowledge.

Not surprisingly, Transhumanism has some quasi-religious aspirations. Although few transhumanists would likely admit it, their theories about the future are a secular outgrowth of Christian eschatology. They believe that something like nanotechnology would allow us to remake Earth into a terrestrial paradise, and from there we would migrate to space, transforming other planets. Our powers, in short, would be limitless. Some transhumanists even fantasize about travelling the universe eternally as near god-like machines. Whereas the Christian view holds out the promise of a City of God apart from an earthly, compromised one, Transhumanism promises a betterment of the human world itself, by developing and making widely available technologies to eliminate aging and to greatly enhance human intellectual, physical, and psychological capacities. Its goal is to escape the confines of being human.

Then there is another serious criticism that comes in particular from religious quarters. The accusation is that Transhumanists attempt to substitute themselves for God. Their ultimate goal is to shape humanity in their own image—the abolition of man in exchange for the rise of super-man. They wrongly claim—in the words of the 2002 Vatican statement *Communion and Stewardship: Human Persons Created in the Image of God*—that "man has full right of disposal over his own biological nature." In contrast to their radical promises—indefinite life extension or the abolition of suffering—Christians attain these in the afterlife. In this view, Transhumanism is just another representative of the long line of utopian movements which seek to create "heaven on earth." For Transhumanism, the sky is the limit—which means there is no real limit. But we may have to revise this view. No longer is the sky the limit, but Heaven is.

This is probably also what makes the transhumanist movement so seductive, according to Meghan O'Gieblyn. It promises to restore, through science, the transcendent hopes that science itself has eliminated. Transhumanists do not believe in the existence of a soul, but they are not strict materialists either. Kurzweil, for instance, claims he believes in "a pattern of matter and energy that persists over time." These patterns, which contain what we tend to think of as our identity, can at least in theory be transferred onto supercomputers, robotic surrogates, or human clones. It's not the same as a soul, of course, but at the very least, it suggests that there is some essential core of our being that will survive and perhaps transcend the inevitable degradation of flesh. That has certainly a semi-religious ring to it.

Probably the most damaging criticism is that Transhumanism is just a new cloak for an older idea: the "nuts-and-bolts" approach of the human body. This idea has become better known as *Mechanicism*—a philosophical doctrine declaring that all living beings, including human beings, are only and merely machine-like automata, which just follow all the physical laws of the Universe. Humans are seen as machines that run with clockwork precision, controlled by the machinery of their bodies. Because this assumes that the only factors operating in living systems are physico-chemical factors, Mechanicism is basically a form of Materialism (see Chapter 10) applied to living beings, but then with something like a "machine-like effect."

Seen in this light, it is easy to conclude that if the combo Mechanicism and Materialism can account and explain so much of the Universe, why not push it to its logical conclusion? Why not make this the complete principle of interpreting the whole of the Universe including ourselves?

That is basically also an old idea, probably best known from the French physician and philosopher Julien de La Mettrie who wrote a book entitled *Man a Machine* (1748). But the idea is older than that. We find it already in 1637 when René Descartes argued that the world is like a machine, its pieces like clockwork mechanisms, and that the machine could be understood by taking its pieces apart, studying them, and then putting them back together to see the larger mechanism again. It is that "nuts-and-bolts" approach we mentioned earlier.

Soon it became common practice to apply this technique to any kind of scientific study—not only in the physical sciences, but also in the life sciences, and even in the social sciences. This technique became so popular and so successful that more and more scientists began to believe that Mechanicism is the only way of understanding their object of study. So it is probably no coincidence that many discoveries about the working of the human body were inspired by the latest technological contraptions of the time. As a matter of fact, our understanding of many human organs came in the form of machine-like mechanisms. The camera with its lens helped us understand the working of the human eye. Bellows clarified how the lungs can do their work. Pumps revealed what the heart does for blood circulation. Computers threw some light on the working of the brain. In line with this, food is to the body what fuel does to the steam-engine. No wonder then, when things go wrong, we use technological devices to correct them: lenses, hearing aids, pace makers, and prostheses. In all these examples, the case could be made that technology was an important driving force for scientific advancement. It can even be stated that science has profited more from the steam engine than the steam engine from science.

Although most scientists nowadays won't publicly declare

themselves defenders of Mechanicism, they are exclusively interested in material entities and the interaction of physical and chemical factors. They may not consider a human being as a real machine, but at least as some kind of mechanism. Even in healthcare, they think of a human being as a machine-like mechanism that needs to be "repaired" if it isn't working properly, so we can fix or replace parts of it as if they were parts of a machine. Thus we lose sight of the "whole" in favor of its mechanical "parts," because the "whole" is considered nothing more than the sum total of its material parts; only the parts are believed to be "real," and the rest is considered fiction. Thus we end up with the monopoly of molecules—or atoms, if you want to go farther "down" the ladder of entities. And Transhumanists faithfully follow this line of thinking.

Before we continue this discussion, it needs to be admitted first that Mechanicism has given us a successful method of studying and analyzing nature. The *model* of a machine can be a helpful tool to better understand the working of an organism. Models simplify what is considered complex, and thus they make such complexity more accessible, controllable, and manageable. There is nothing wrong with studying an organism as a machine—the success of the machinery model proves it. But this harmless technique becomes dangerous when we claim next that an organism "is nothing but" a machine. However, regardless of how well mechanistic models explain the workings of a human body, a human being *is* not a machine. Looking at an organism *as if* it were a machine does not *make* it a machine.

Let's move on from Transhumanism to Tech-Utopianism—which is in search of "a machine that can far surpass all the intellectual activities of any man however clever," in the words of I. J. Good. It is Mechanicism that connects the two. We are entering here the field of Artificial Intelligence (further abbreviated to *AI*). John McCarthy, who coined the term AI in 1955, defines it as "the science and engineering of making intelligent machines." But AI claims go much further than what a personal computer, or even a robot, can do. Its central claim is that a central property of humans—their intelligence—can be described so precisely that a machine can be built to simulate it.

However, the idea that a machine can simulate human intelligence raises many philosophical issues, especially as to what is meant by "human intelligence." If we take "intelligence" as more than processing information—something a robot can do too—but also in the sense of the mind's capacity of "thinking," the question becomes: Would an appropriately programmed computer with the right inputs and outputs just *simulate* a mind, or actually *have* a mind? The former part of the question, simulating a mind, is relatively neutral, but the latter part, having a mind, would have enormous philosophical repercussions, if it were true.

The position of the latter part is often called "strong AI." It was already behind some of the statements of early AI researchers. For example, in 1955, AI founder Herbert Simon declared that we can explain now "how a system composed of matter can have the properties of mind." Cognitive scientist John Haugeland went as far as writing that "we are, at root, computers ourselves." More specifically, one could state that strong AI, in David Cole's words, represents the view that suitably programmed computers can understand natural language and actually have other mental capabilities similar to the humans whose abilities they mimic.

One of the leading attacks against these more extravagant claims comes from the Berkeley philosopher John Searle. He introduced what is widely known now as the "Chinese Room Argument"—first presented in 1983. Over the last three decades, this argument was the subject of many discussions.

In January 1990, the popular monthly *Scientific American* took the debate to a general scientific audience.

Searle himself summarized the Chinese Room argument as follows: Imagine a native English speaker who knows no Chinese locked in a room full of boxes of Chinese symbols (a data base) together with a book of instructions for manipulating the symbols (the program). Imagine that people outside the room send in Chinese symbols which, unknown to the person in the room, are questions in Chinese (the input). And imagine that by following the instructions in the program, the man in the room is able to pass out Chinese symbols which are correct answers to the questions (the output). Then, Searle asserts, this program enables the person in the room to pass the so-called Turing Test for understanding Chinese, yet that person does not understand a word of Chinese.

The question Searle wants to answer is this: Does the machine literally "understand" Chinese? Or is it merely simulating the ability to understand Chinese? If you can carry on an intelligent conversation with an unknown partner, does this imply your statements are really "understood"? The position of strong AI would claim such is indeed the case. In contrast, Searle argues that what the machine is doing cannot be described as "understanding," and therefore, the machine does not have a "mind" in anything like the normal sense of the word. A computer can translate language—as several translator tools online show us—but the computer does not really understand language, let alone think of itself as an "I" who does the understanding. Hence, Searle concludes, strong AI is mistaken.

What Searle means by "understanding" is what some philosophers call "intentionality"—the property of being about something, of having content. It is the "mystery" of how mental thoughts about objects come to be *about* those objects. Unquestionably, thoughts are about something beyond themselves. To use an analogy, anything that shows up on a computer monitor remains just an "empty" collection of "ones and zeros" that do not point beyond themselves until some kind of human interpretation gives sense and meaning to the code and interprets it as being "about" something. Think of what we call a picture: It may carry information, but the picture itself is just a piece of paper that makes "sense" only when human beings interpret the picture as being "about" something else. The same with books: They provide lots of information for "book worms," but to real worms they only have paper to offer. That's where the need for intentionality and about-ness comes in. This raises the question whether a computer really "understands" what it is doing. It manipulates symbols or numbers that mean something to the human programmer, but do they mean anything to the computer? Does it "know" that the string of symbols it prints out refers to books, for instance, rather than to melons or planets?

If this objection is true, then understanding information must be more than merely making use of that information, otherwise we would end up with bizarre conclusions. The physicist Stephen Barr makes the following comparison:

> An ordinary door lock has "information" mechanically encoded within it that allows it to distinguish a key of the right shape from keys of other shapes. ... Does the lock understand anything? Most sensible people would say not. The lock does not understand shapes any more than the fish understand shapes. Neither of them can understand a universal concept.

As a matter of fact, universal concepts are uniquely human. Whereas the brain can handle signals and images, it seems that only the human mind can deal with concepts. Images can have some degree of generality—we can visualize a circle without imagining any specific size—whereas concepts have a universality that images can never have—the concept "circle" applies to every circle without exception. Because images are inherently ambiguous, open to various interpretations, we need concepts to give them a specific interpretation. That's how mental concepts transform "things" of the world into "objects" of knowledge, thus enabling humans to see with their "mental eyes" what no physical eyes could ever see.

A concept may be as simple as a "circle" or as complex as a "gene," but a concept definitely goes beyond what the senses provide. Concepts are not perceived images. Images are by nature ambiguous, open to various interpretations; so we need concepts to interpret them. We do not "see" genes but have come to hypothesize and conceptualize them with a concept. We do not even see circles, for a "circle" is a highly abstract, idealized concept (with a radius and diameter). We can even conceptualize something that we cannot visualize— something like a circle with four dimensions, for instance. Once these concepts have been established and mastered, we have become "regular observers" of "circles" and "genes." But again, these are not images but concepts.

Our criticism of "strong IA" could even go further. Machines only exist because they have a human maker. A computer can be programmed to make decisions with an if-then-else structure, for instance. But this does not mean that the computer actually deliberates and decides—programmers did, and they make it look like the machine does too. The "reason" why a calculator adds or a pump pumps is that a machine was designed for that purpose—and not because it "intends" to. Machines don't have purposes but humans do. In other words, computers only do what we, human beings with a mind, cause them to do, for we have proven to be champion machine builders.

Because of this, all AI systems presume a designing mind. The parts of a robot do not come together on their own and function as a robot, but have to be arranged by a designing mind to do so. To put this in a catchphrase, not only is there "a machine in the man," but there is also "a man in the machine" who designed the machine. So the popular slogan "Man versus Machine" should actually read "Man versus Man"—versus the Man who built the machine. Are these considerations final and decisive? Perhaps not, but they cannot just be ignored either. Only time will tell what AI is capable of creating, but that should not stop us from asking some critical questions.

Some side effects of Transhumanism

Transhumanism has also affected the way we think about morality (see Chapter 6). Obviously, morality is at stake here. Scientific knowledge often seems to have the potential to cut both ways—good effects and bad effects. The same holds for technology—it can be used for good as well as evil purposes. Even something as simple as the use of fire can be beneficial for humanity (cooking, etc.) as well as detrimental to humanity (burning, etc.).

This makes the outcome of new technology often unpredictable. This unpredictability can be used in three different ways: in a defensive way by claiming, "Nobody could have foreseen those risks!"; in an offensive way by saying, "You never can tell, so try it!"; or in a preventive way by warning, "You never can tell, so never do it!" These viewpoints are extreme and one-sided. Optimists see a possibility in every difficulty; they gaze into their crystal ball and see a bright future. Pessimists, on the other hand, see a difficulty in every possibility; they predict a gloomy future and warn us. However, our choice is not simply between doom or utopia. But no matter how we look at it, we cannot avoid a *moral* assessment. Transhumanists seem to miss, or rather avoid, this point.

Transhumanism usually declares that everything that is technologically possible is, automatically and at the same time, morally permissible. In their view, technology determines morality. But that would be detrimental to morality. In this view, it has become a servant of technology: whatever is possible is therefore permissible. There would no longer be independent, absolute, timeless moral rules to determine what is morally right and what is morally wrong.

There is a similar discussion about the role of morality in science. Nazi-doctors such as Joseph Mengele, for instance, show us what happens when morality does not control their scientific research. Therefore, science cannot monitor morality, but it is rather the other way around—morality ought to control science instead. Albert Einstein was right when he spoke of "the moral foundations of science, but you cannot turn around and speak of the scientific foundations of morality." Morality can interrogate science, but science cannot question morality—morality is beyond its reach.

There are two very different ways of looking at "good science." Science can be "good" judged by methodological criteria (good-for-the-purpose), but it can also be "good" judged by moral criteria (good-as-such). In the case of methodological criteria we are dealing with relative rules or norms; they indicate whether a certain kind of science is good in terms of current methodological criteria. "Good" science in this sense is "methodologically sound" science. However, there also exists "good" science in another sense—

in relation to certain moral rules and values, that is. Science practiced in Nazi camps was not "good" science in moral terms, although it may have been methodologically sound. That's where a moral assessment is needed.

Something similar holds for the relationship between technology and morality: morality should rule what is allowed in technology. So morality should direct technology, and not the other way around. Technology, as well as science, should feel responsible when it comes to morality. However, that's not always what happens. As the philosopher of science Jerome Ravetz put it in a rather sarcastic way: "Science takes the credit for penicillin, while Society takes the blame for the Bomb." Transhumanists like to blame others when it suits them. When there are bad effects, though, both science and technology should take the blame. Scientists and technologists cannot hide themselves in an "ivory tower."

All these considerations would plead for a professional code in science and technology. Perhaps scientists and technologists need a professional code similar to the Hippocratic oath in the medical profession. Especially scientists working in biological specialties are badly in need of a professional oath, as biological knowledge and technology have given them great powers which have an influence on many value-laden issues that go to the very core of human existence. Scientists have to face the fact that the outcome of their work is to alter much of what ordinary folk hold dear. The issues range from medical and genetic research to questions about how to control life and death.

A few proposals have been made regarding an oath for life scientists. One of them runs as follows:

*I pledge to put my knowledge completely at
the service of humankind. I shall prosecute my*

profession conscientiously and with dignity. I shall never collaborate in research aimed at the unjustified extermination of living organisms or the disturbance of the biological equilibrium which is harmful to humankind, neither shall I support such research in any way. The aim of my scientific work will be the promotion of the common welfare of humankind, and in this context I shall not kill organisms nor shall I allow the killing of organisms for inferior, short-sighted, opportunistic reasons. I accept responsibility for unforeseen, harmful results directly originating from my work; I shall undo these results as far as lies in my power. This I vow voluntarily and on my word of honor.

An oath like this would also be important for Transhumanists. Perhaps it would be able to curb the power fantasies of technologists who dream of a "brave new world," without any moral restrictions and responsibilities.

Given all of the above, we must come to the conclusion that Transhumanism is a doctrine which is not only seriously limited but also very destructive.

14. Evolutionism

What is Evolutionism?

Evolutionism is a doctrine pretending that *all* of life, more in particular all of *human* life, can be explained in evolutionary terms. The doctrine of Evolutionism is based on evolutionary theory, which was launched by Charles Darwin and thus became almost immediately known as Darwinism. Soon after Darwin's death, the Mendelian principles of inheritance were brought together with the Darwinian principles of evolution, which started a new field that has become known as Modern Evolutionary Synthesis—often referred to as Neo-Darwinism. The (very basic) basics of the modern evolutionary theory are as follows.

1. Organisms of a population are genetically different from each other. Genetic diversity (or variation or variability) is essential for evolution. If all organisms of a population were genetically identical to each other, evolution would be impossible.

2. Genetic differences are caused by mutations, which change the genetic material, more specifically the genetic DNA code.

3. Mutations are random events. They happen at random, hit genetic material randomly, and have a random effect. Mutations are the main source of genetic variability.

4. Genetic differences cause differences in chances of reproduction and survival. Some genetic differences enhance the chances of reproduction and survival, while others worsen those chances. This is referred to as "natural selection."

5. Natural selection promotes genetic differences to different degrees. Natural selection promotes "good" genetic designs more so than "bad" genetic designs, which makes them increase their frequency in future generations. This is also commonly referred to as "survival of the fittest." Unlike mutations, which are considered to happen at random, natural selection is highly "selective."

Whether this evolutionary theory is in fact sustainable or adequate is beyond the scope of this book. The question here is how the doctrine of Evolutionism deals with this theory.

First of all, it considers evolutionary theory a reliable, tested, and correct scientific theory. But then, and that's the kicker, it declares this theory completely adequate to explain not only *all* of life but also, or more specifically, all of *human* life. Everything in human life, every aspect of human life, is supposed to be entirely the outcome of an evolutionary process. This means, for instance, that human rationality and human morality are also the mere result of an evolutionary process, based on genetics and natural selection.

But evolutionism goes much further than that. It uses the randomness of mutations to declare all of evolution as a matter of pure *chance* and "blind" luck. That's when "survival of the fittest" boils down to "survival of the luckiest." Chance is considered "blind," because it has no "favorites," no memory, and no foresight. Consequently, biologists in the camp of Evolutionism take something like DNA as a random product of evolution, based on random mutations. Perhaps the best known representative of this view is the biologist Richard Dawkins who made chance and randomness into a capricious, blind agent, almost a deity, or a "blind watchmaker" at best, according to the title of one of his books.

Well, if it is indeed "chance" that ultimately drives evolution, then there is no space left for some goal or direction or *purpose* in evolution. Indeed, there is no purpose or direction to randomness or chance; if you do not believe this, just test it at a slot machine. The fact that natural selection does have a direction does not obliterate the fact that mutations do not. Therefore, supporters of Evolutionism see no purpose at all in evolution. One of them, the biologist Douglas Futuyama put it this way: "[W]e need not invoke, nor can we find any evidence for, any design, goal, or purpose anywhere in the natural world." The late paleontologist George Gaylord Simpson had already said in more provocative terms that "man is the result of a purposeless and natural process that did not have him in mind." Richard Dawkins joins them when he states that biology is about "things that give the appearance of having been designed for a purpose." That's all there is to it, in his view—merely an "appearance." He also says, "Natural selection is the blind watchmaker, blind because it does not see ahead, does not plan consequences, has no purpose in view."

Not only does Evolutionism reject the idea that the Universe is purpose-driven, but it also denies there is any *design* in nature whatsoever. Although Dawkins, for instance, sees in evolution "the appearance of having been designed for a purpose," he considers that a deceptive appearance. In his own words, "So powerful is the illusion of design, it took humanity until the mid-19th century to realize that it is an illusion."

That we quoted Dawkins so often is because he more explicitly than others adheres to Evolutionism—something most biologists do only tacitly, or even oblivious. Dawkins expresses a rather wide-spread view among biologists when he says, "The Universe we observe has precisely the properties we should expect if there is, at bottom, no design, no purpose, no evil and no good, nothing but blind pitiless indifference." How widely accepted this doctrine is became very visible when 38 Nobel laureates issued a statement in 2005 defending Darwin's theory with the words, "evolution is understood to be the result of an unguided and unplanned process of random variation and natural selection."

In all these cases, a scientific theory, evolutionary theory, has been transformed into a doctrine, Evolutionism, which pretends to be the only valid and all-inclusive explanation of life, especially human life, by claiming superiority, or even a monopoly, over any additional explanations.

What is wrong with Evolutionism?

Probably the most damaging attack on Evolutionism is that it is self-destructive. Interestingly enough, even Charles Darwin himself vaguely acknowledged this problem when he said in his *Autobiography*, "But then with me the horrid doubt always arises whether the convictions of man's mind, which has been developed from the mind of the lower animals, are of any value or at all trustworthy. Would anyone trust in the convictions of a monkey's mind, if there are any convictions in such a mind?" The theory of natural selection makes him wonder whether, as he puts it, "[T]he mind of man, which has, as I fully believe, been developed from a mind as low as that possessed by the lowest animal, [can] be trusted when it draws such grand conclusions." Darwin had good reason to worry about this "horrid doubt."

What Darwin did not seem to realize is that the theory of natural selection can neither create nor explain the rationality of the human mind, but must assume it. If the human mind were really the mere product of natural selection, so would be the science of evolution, as well as Evolutionism—hence nothing we claim to know could then be trusted. It is rather obvious that the rationality of a person such as Darwin, who discovered the theory of evolutionary theory, or of scientists such as Watson and Crick, who discovered the structure of DNA in genes, must be more than that which they discovered. Otherwise their discoveries would be mere illusions concocted by a neural network under the shaky direction of genes shaped by natural selection.

What can we conclude from this? Instead of claiming that our rationality comes from "below"—from the animal world, based on genes and natural selection—it is much more likely it comes from "Above" where God's Rationality reigns. Human rationality is a reflection of God's Rationality. That's where its power comes from. And that's another reason why Evolutionism is flawed. It is an assault not only on our own rationality but also on God's rationality as reflected in creation (see Chapter 12).

But there are many more problems with Evolutionism. They have something to do with the fact that Evolutionism declares that everything in (human) life is without a plan, without a purpose, and without a design. Let's discuss these three issues one by one.

No plan, really? The idea that evolution is steered by randomness, and therefore is without any plan, is based on the fact that mutations are random. However, how are we to understand randomness? The word "random" is a scientific, actually a statistical or stochastic, concept. When people toss a coin, there is randomness involved because the outcome is independent of what the one who tosses the coin would like to see happening, and it is also independent of previous and future tosses. However, in the context of mutations, the term "random" has a more specific, technical meaning. When biologists say that mutations are "statistically random"—they mean mutations just happen one way or the other, but there is no direct connection with other events such as environmental changes or immediate and future needs, so the former do not affect the latter, nor the other way around. Therefore, they say, there is no "plan" behind randomness or chance, because chance has no "favorites," no "memory," and no "fore-sight."

So far so good, for "randomness" in science is merely a statistical, stochastic concept—a concept that can be scientifically tested for. So when we speak of randomness in science, we are talking in statistical terms, in the sense of how things in this Universe are related to each other, and how they are not related to each other.

But that technical meaning changes dramatically when supporters of Evolutionism interpret the word "random" as "without plan." At that moment they are leaving scientific territory, for their interpretation would change life into a mere play of whimsical and fortuitous events. By so doing, they turn "chance" and "randomness" into a capricious, blind agent—the deity of randomness versus the God of order. Randomness is a scientific term that tells us is that causes can be independent of each other. But when, instead, randomness becomes a matter of "luck," of "good or bad luck," its meaning changes dramatically. Whereas random-ness and chance describe the relationship *between* causes, luck or fortune is a worldview notion that supposedly refers to some kind of agency *beyond* the realm of regular causes— which is no longer a scientific issue.

Yet, some scientists keep falling for the timeless temptation to capitalize the word "chance" by changing it into the goddess of Fate or Doom or Blind Fate. By doing so, they slip from a theory about evolution into a dogma of

Evolutionism. However, science has nothing to say about chance with a capital C. Fate is far beyond its reach, for it is in essence a worldview notion, not a scientific one. In the words of the particle physicist Stephen Barr, "one must distinguish between words used by scientists and words used scientifically." Scientists can speak scientifically about randomness but not about Fate, Fortune, or Luck. No matter how biologists believe evolution operates, chance with a capital C is beyond their reach and expertise, for they cannot speak about it scientifically.

What supporters of evolutionism are actually doing is making "Chance" the ultimate primary cause of this Universe, thus changing randomness into a cause that needs no further explanation. However, if randomness is the basis for change in the Universe, then it must be a secondary cause and cannot be itself a primary cause (see Chapter 3). Instead it is God, the Primary Cause, who is the ultimate cause of randomness in nature, including the emergence of mutations. When speaking of randomness in science, we are talking in statistical terms, in the sense of how things in this Universe are related to each other—not how they are related to a Higher Power, God. When it comes to God, randomness has lost its meaning. So there could still very well be a "plan" behind it all. St. Padre Pio was apt to say in various ways that it is God who arranges the coincidences. As a matter of fact, Thomas Aquinas once said, "Whoever believes that everything is a matter of chance, does not believe that God exists."

No purpose, really? It is true that, in science, there is no room for purpose-talk. Although the word "purpose" can have several meanings, it is often understood as a synonym for the word "intention." Well, the concept of "purpose" in the sense of "intention" does not belong in science and was taken out of science. It was taken out of astronomy by

Nicolaus Copernicus, out of physics by Isaac Newton, and out of biology by Charles Darwin. Astronomers do not seek the purpose of comets or supernovas, nor do chemists search for the purpose or intention of hydrogen bonds. The sun does not rise every morning because it "intends" to, but because it follows physical laws. Water "seeks" its own level, but it does not do so intentionally. Eye patterns on butterfly wings have the effect of warning enemies; that is a function of eye patterns, but not a purpose or intention of butterflies. The concept of purpose plays no role in scientific explanations of how causes are related to each other.

However, if purposes do not belong in science, one cannot jump to the conclusion that there is no purpose in life at all, let alone in relationship to God. Scientists have to face the problem that they cannot make statements like these in their role as scientists. First they eliminate the concept of purpose from science, but then they keep using it in order to reject it. Once "purpose" has been eliminated from science, it can no longer be used, let alone be explained, by science, as it is from now on no longer part of scientific vocabulary. That is why it is most striking to see how defenders of Evolutionism still make it their main purpose in life to claim that there are no purposes in life at all.

There are actually strong indications that purposes cannot possibly be removed entirely from human discourse. When scientists removed "purposes" from scientific discourse, they removed them as secondary causes, but they left their reference to the Primary Cause untouched. So they did not make purposes disappear completely; they just moved them from inside to outside the scientific domain—from the context of secondary causes to the context of the Primary Cause.

Those who keep denying the existence of any purposes at all need to ask themselves some pertinent philosophical questions. If there is no purpose in the Universe, tout court, how then were we ever to know there is no such thing as a purpose? As C. S. Lewis put it, "if there were no light in the Universe and therefore no creatures with eyes, we would never know it was dark." Besides, we should ask those who deny the existence of purposes what the purpose is of trying to prove or claim that there is no purpose in life. As a matter of fact, denying that there are purposes in life defeats its own claim. The reason is simple: If it is your purpose to remove all purposes from life, then you are also wiping out your own purpose of doing so. Those whose purpose it is to eradicate all purposes from life have obviously lost even the very purpose of acting that way.

In a Universe without purposes, there could not even be any man-made machines, since such machines, curiously enough, are always made for a purpose; the world of technology is per definition purpose-driven, based on purposes that designers and engineers have in mind (see Chapter 13). Therefore, we could never ban purposes from the Universe by saying the Universe is just a machine which runs with clockwork precision, as some scientists have tried. So purposes are still standing tall, in spite of Evolutionism's claims.

No design, really? It is often said that Darwin took "design" out of evolution. Before him, William Paley's natural theology had been popular in speaking of a "Watch-Maker," a design-Designer. Even the young Darwin could accept that, but soon the older Darwin would change his mind. George Bernard Shaw once said that Charles Darwin had thrown William Paley's "watch" into the ocean. Well, what Darwin did throw away was Paley's "watchmaker," but certainly not his legendary watch; if he did throw anything away, it was Paley's design-Designer, but certainly not the design concept itself.

As a matter of fact, the concept of "design" is an artifact analogy that is as basic to Darwin's evolutionary theory as it is to Paley's natural theology. Since the heart has a design like a pump, it is a successful design that works "in order to" or "for the sake of" circulating blood—which makes it a great target for natural selection. If it did not have that design, the heart would not work. Michael Ruse, a philosopher of biology, was right when he said that after Darwin, the heart still existed "for" circulation; the cause of its existence may have been different, but its design features were not. As strange as it may sound, Darwin put "design" and "usefulness" back into the picture, but in a veiled way. His evolutionary theory still requires some kind of design. If the heart had a different design, it might no longer be "successful" in the "battle for survival." Natural selection works per definition on cases with a "successful" design.

We need to realize there are two sides to being successful. A biological design can only be successful if it is in accordance with the "cosmic design," the design of the Universe which includes the laws of nature. Without this cosmic design, biological designs could not work at all. A heart could not pump blood if it did not follow hydrodynamic laws; a bird's wing would not let the bird fly if it did not follow aerodynamic laws; fish could not swim if their design did not follow hydrodynamic laws. These laws are part of the cosmic design. It is the *cosmic* design that explains which *biological* designs are successful in reproduction and survival—as much so as the cosmic design regulates which bridges are successful technological designs, and which are failures.

Given the cosmic design, some biological designs are "better" than others in having a "better outcome" than others—a better "fit," so to speak. They must have "something" in their biological design that carried them through the "filter" of natural selection. Natural selection can only select those specific biological designs that are in accordance with the rules and laws of the cosmic design. Natural selection does not *explain* a "fit" but *uses* a "fit" in order to select what fits best.

Even Darwin himself always felt uneasy about his term "natural selection," because it leads almost automatically to the obvious question of "Selection by whom or by what?" Indeed, the implication of a "selecting agent" is looming large. Yet, in many passages, Darwin referred to "nature," some kind of feminine deity, as the agent of selection. Eventually, his colleague Alfred Wallace convinced Darwin to replace the term "natural selection" with Spencer's notion of "survival of the fittest" in the 5th edition of his book. Nevertheless, the question of "Selection by whom or by what," remains pressing. Although Darwin wanted to avoid this question, there is in fact an answer for it: selection is done through the cosmic design.

Let's bring this discussion to a conclusion. Defenders of Evolutionism have no right and no reason in their role of scientists to decree that we as human beings are unintended, unplanned, unguided, fortuitous creatures, or mere products of a blind and purposeless fate, for claiming that goes far beyond their competence as scientists. Science has nothing to say about such issues. As Stephen Barr rightly remarks, "When biologists start making statements about processes being unsupervised, undirected, unguided, and unplanned, they are not speaking scientifically." Evolutionary theory cannot even explain why there is evolution to begin with.

Some side effects of Evolutionism

Starting with natural selection and "survival of the fittest," it is only a small step to Spencer's idea that human society is an arena of struggle in which the fittest survive. This paved the way for the idea that "supremacists" should survive, at the cost of "misfits." This idea soon became the cornerstone of eugenics—the study and practice of selective breeding applied to humans, with the aim of actively improving the human gene pool. Eugenics basically asserts that we should breed humans like we breed animals, hence we should be able to kill them like we kill animals—for we are reportedly just animals, and nothing more.

The "interventions" advocated and practiced by eugenicists involved a wide range of "degenerates" or "unfits"—the poor, the blind, the mentally ill, entire "racial" groups such as Jews, Blacks, Roma ("Gypsies"). All of these were deemed "unfit" to live according to their despotic dogma called "survival of the fittest." And this, in turn, led to practices such as segregation, sterilization, genocide, preemptive abortions, euthanasia, designer babies, and in the extreme case of Nazi Germany, mass extermination. G.B. Shaw once predicted that "part of eugenic politics would finally land us in an extensive use of the lethal chamber."

Is it fair to blame Darwin for these developments? Yes, he might at least carry part of the blame. Let's not forget that the full title of his first and famous book was *On the Origin of Species by Means of Natural Selection, or the Preservation of Favoured Races in the Struggle for Life*. The words "Preservation of Favoured Races" do not sound very scientific. Darwin may have started his career on the right path, but gradually went more and more off track in his claims. He came to say he had found no fundamental difference between man and the higher mammals in their mental and moral faculties; he considered their morals and minds deeply rooted in the animal world. All that humans have and are, whether physically, mentally, or spiritually, had to come from the animal world in Darwin's view. By the time Darwin published the second edition of *The Descent of Man* in 1874, he had added Francis Galton's eugenic theories and the social philosophy of Herbert Spencer's "survival of the fittest" to the mix. He also called Spencer "our greatest philosopher," and declared *Hereditary Genius*, Galton's treatise on the biological nature of intelligence and moral character, "remarkable."

Darwin may not have directly promoted eugenics, but he surely prepared the way for it. As a matter of fact, his immediate family would soon be involved in that movement—his sons George and Leonard became active in promoting eugenics, with Leonard serving as president of the Eugenics Education Society, the main eugenics group in Great Britain. And Darwin's cousin, Francis Galton, would become the founder of the "eugenics crusade." Darwin himself had already complained about how "the reckless, degraded, and often vicious members of society, tend to increase at a quicker rate than the provident and generally virtuous members"—although he admittedly did add, "if we were intentionally to neglect the weak and helpless, it could only be for a contingent benefit, with an overwhelming present evil."

Later in life, Darwin would return to this issue during his last conversations with Alfred Russel Wallace, in which he spoke "very gloomily on the future of humanity" because "in our modern civilization natural selection had no play, and the fittest did not survive." In his book *The Descent of Man*, Darwin even claimed that the break between apes and man in evolution fell "between the negro or Australian and the gorilla." This allegation about blacks as belonging to "a more primitive stage of human evolution" soon became a powerful scientific rationale for racist public policies.

An important propagandist of eugenics was the founder of the Planned Parenthood Federation of America: Margaret

Higgins Sanger, a radical feminist, eugenicist, and Marxist—still the hero of many present-day abortion activists. Her statements, mostly published in her own magazine and some books, are horrendous, although mostly passed over by her followers nowadays. Here is a selection of her horrifying statements: "The most merciful thing that a large family does to one of its infant members is to kill it." The purpose in promoting birth control is "to create a race of thoroughbreds." And, "We do not want word to go out that we want to exterminate the Negro population." She also wrote that couples should be required to submit applications to have a child, for she detested the fact that "anyone, no matter how ignorant, how diseased mentally or physically, how lacking in all knowledge of children, seemed to consider he or she had the right to become a parent." It is hard to believe that all of this could ever have been put on paper, yet Planned Parenthood did not stray far from what its founder, Sanger, had once proclaimed.

At the beginning of the previous century, eugenics flourished, not only at universities and on the editorial boards of scientific journals, but also in politics. The Virginia Justice Oliver Wendell Holmes declared in Buck v. Bell (1927) that "three generations of imbeciles are enough," and launched a massive campaign of state-enforced sterilizations, thinking that America's salvation could be found in "blocking the lower classes from breeding." Interestingly enough, the one dissenting vote to Holmes's decision was cast by the sole Catholic on the court, Pierce Butler.

Perhaps eugenics is only a side effect of evolutionism, but it contrasts sharply with Catholicism. Eugenics places the final end of human beings in their biological "worth," but Catholic teaching places it in eternal life. Put differently, the Church makes human culture subordinate to morality, whereas eugenics makes morality a mere product of human culture. Although eugenics did not develop directly from evolutionary theory itself, it is definitely an offshoot of Evolutionism. In Evolutionism, there is no good or bad. In regard to issues such as slavery, abortion, or genocide, Evolutionism can only talk in terms of "winners" and "losers," because the concepts of "good" and "bad" are not only outside its scope but are even declared illusory. That is why eugenics eventually dehumanizes, leading to what C. S. Lewis called "the abolition of man." As Pope John Paul II observed, "When the sense of God is lost, there is also a tendency to lose the sense of man, of his dignity and life."

Given all of the above, we must come to the conclusion that evolutionism is a doctrine which is not only seriously flawed but also very destructive.

15. Atheism

What is Atheism?

Atheism is not a homogenous kind of doctrine. In its most general form, it proclaims the theory that God does not exist, but it comes with at least four different kinds of "flavors":

1. We *don't* know if God exists.
2. We *cannot* know if God exists.
3. We don't *care* to know if God exists.
4. We don't *want* to know if God exists.

The first kind—"we *don't* know"—can be found among so-called agnostics. Although agnosticism is not a form of atheism in the literal, strict sense, it comes at least close to atheism, because agnostics are ambivalent: They neither believe nor disbelieve in the existence of God. The label of agnosticism may have been a recent invention—a word that the biologist Thomas H. Huxley invented—but the idea behind it is much older. Diogenes Laërtius said already in the 3rd century AD, "As to the gods, I have no means of knowing either that they exist or do not exist."

Agnosticism nowadays applies this idea about "gods" in paganism to the Christian notion of "God"—which is quite a stretch. It asserts that we just do not know whether God exists or not, and what is worse, we presumably have no way of ever knowing one way or the other (at least not before we die). In that sense, agnosticism is not really atheism, for it also says that we have no way of knowing that God does *not* exist. It just keeps agnostics in limbo; they neither deny nor affirm God's existence.

Agnostics swear by logic, and they claim that logic cannot demonstrate the *falsity* of a belief in God (it is said to be an unbeatable, unverifiable hypothesis), but neither can it demonstrate the *truth* of a belief in God (it is said to be a daring, undecided hypothesis). This makes the biologist Julian Huxley exclaim, "We should be agnostic about those things for which there is no evidence." Agnostics think that they are not taking any stand pro-or-con at all and therefore that they are safe, secure, and invulnerable to any attacks. That must be a comforting thought to them!

Again, are agnostics atheists? Yes and no. The agnostic says, "I don't have a *knowledge* that God exists." The atheist says, "I don't have a *belief* that God exists." You can say both things at the same time. Some agnostics are atheistic and some are theistic. Agnosticism is not a belief system the way atheism is; rather, it is a theory of knowledge. An atheist denies the existence of God; an agnostic professes ignorance about God's existence. For the latter, God may exist, but in their view, reason can neither prove nor disprove it. So agnosticism keeps people undecided.

The second kind of atheism—"we *cannot* know if God exists"—can be found among supporters of Scientism (see Chapter 12). In their view, there is no way God can be known with any degree of certainty—not so much because God is in essence beyond human reach, but because there is no space for God in scientific vocabulary. This makes God a "nothing," at best an illusion or delusion. Because "God" is a concept that cannot be empirically tested and verified, God-talk is *ipso facto* meaningless.

These atheists claim that in order to prove there is a God, we need either empirical proof or logical proof for the existence of God—proof beyond any doubt. Stephen Hawking, for instance, thinks along these lines as he exclaims, "When people ask me if a god created the Universe, I tell them that the question itself makes no sense." Atheists in this category proclaim that there cannot be any *empirical* proof, because God is not accessible to our senses, so he is not measurable, quantifiable, or touchable. Sam Harris takes a similar position: "The faith of religion is belief on insufficient evidence."

Although atheism is commonly understood to be about the absence of *belief* in God, most atheists of this kind will say it is about the absence of God himself. They are "positively" sure that God does *not* exist, because they adhere faithfully to the doctrines of positivism, empiricism, and scientism. They reject religion on so-called scientific grounds. You will find this kind of atheism particularly in books of scientists such as Richard Dawkins, Daniel Dennett, E. O. Wilson, Peter Higgs, Carl Sagan, Peter Atkins, Francis Crick, Peter Singer, and Sam Harris. They tell us that believing in God is just impossible because science has shown us there *is* no God. These atheists tend to believe that modern science is on their side. Mark Twain put it in a nutshell: "A man is accepted into a church for what he believes and he is turned out for what he knows." The idea is clear: atheism is based on knowledge; religion is not. When we look through our telescopes or microscopes, we never see God, so we *know* there is no god—on scientific grounds. This view is probably best summarized by the title of one of Dawkins' popular books—*The God Delusion*. That's what God is according to this view—a delusion. Why? Because science tells us so! Of course, it is not science but Scientism that tells us so.

The third kind of atheism—"we don't *care* to know if God exists"—is especially prevalent among supporters of Secularism (see Chapter 4), Humanism (see Chapter 5), Liberalism (see Chapter 6), and Transhumanism (see Chapter 13). In these doctrines, God has become a needless and redundant Entity, because God has lost in the competition with Man. These atheists have no longer any "need" for God. They declare human beings as fully sufficient in themselves, fully self-made, and in complete control of their own history. All our problems—personal, social, technological, and what have you—can be entirely solved by using the right human knowledge, technology, reasoning, and judgment. We are supposed to be in full control of ourselves and should further free ourselves through economic, technological, and social liberation. From then on, not Heaven but the sky is the limit.

The French philosopher Denis Diderot said already during the Enlightenment, "Whether God exists or does not exist, he has come to rank among the most sublime and useless truths." More recently, atheists of this kind have taken a similar position. Isaac Asimov, for instance, expressed as his opinion: "I don't have the evidence to prove that God doesn't exist, but I so strongly suspect he doesn't that I don't want to waste my time." The founder of Microsoft, Bill Gates, put it more directly: "Religion is not very efficient. There's a lot more I could be doing on a Sunday morning."

People who fit in this line of atheism too are those who no longer perceive anything spiritual or religious in their lives; they suffer from some kind of "spiritual amnesia"; they have completely lost their religious dimension. They are not so much atheists as heathens who have never thought about God, or never even heard of God. These people live in a very noisy and busy world, filled with radio and TV, loudspeakers and earphones, which overpower and squash any other thoughts—which turns them into "heathens."

Here we have atheism in its simplest form: We don't care about God because we just never think of God. This form of atheism is not of the theoretical kind that makes one believe there is no God, but rather of the practical type that makes one act as if there is no God. It doesn't deny God, it doesn't fight God, it just *ignores* God. The only thing left in life is the "rock-solid" reality of food, money, sex, and material possessions—all of which will collapse when we die. These atheists are not really non-believers, because they never thought of the possibility there is a God to believe in. Even the word "God" is completely missing in their vocabulary. They just live a life without God, and have no idea of what they are missing.

The fourth kind of atheism—"we don't *want* to know if God exists"—varies from disliking God, at one end, to hating God, at the other end. In this kind of atheism, God is an unwanted and uncalled-for Entity—at best a nuisance. At the one end, we find some believers in Scientism (see Chapter 12). One of them is the philosopher Thomas Nagel: "I want atheism to be true and am uneasy by the fact that some of the most intelligent and well-informed people I know are religious believers. It isn't just that that I don't believe in God and, naturally, hope that I'm right in my belief. It's that I hope there is no God! I don't want there to be a God; I don't want the universe to be like that." One could also say that these atheists don't like the way the world looks to them with God in the picture.

At the other end, we find mostly believers in Materialism (see Chapter 10) and Communism (see Chapter 8). This is the atheism of people who vehemently *renounce* to believe in God and want others to believe that believing in God is "evil" and needs to be attacked or even eradicated. These atheists consider spreading their message of God-hatred to be their "holy war," their "sacred mission," a Jihad against God. This form of atheism does not question God, it does not deny God, it does not neglect God, but it plainly *rejects* God. George Orwell referred to this kind of atheists when he said about someone, "He was an embittered atheist (the sort of atheist who does not so much disbelieve in God as personally dislike Him)."

There is something very peculiar about this form of atheism: it is a kind of hate speech that tries to constantly remind us of God while maintaining God does not exist. How could one dislike, or even hate, something that is not there? Why would one persistently try to prove to people the non-existence of a being that is not supposed to exist anyway? Cardinal Stefan Wyszyński, the late Primate of Poland, who dealt most of his life with the aggressive atheism of Soviet Communism, has an astounding answer to these questions: in order to hate God, you must first have faith that there is a God, for only when you firmly believe in God will you be able to hate him. That was his explanation for the fact that the Communist media in his country used to persistently mention God in their God-less propaganda against God.

In all four cases mentioned above, atheism is true to the original meaning of the word a-theism—"without God." It is a doctrine without God. Atheists may differ in the arguments they use to defend their position, but in some way or another, they *question* or *deny* or *ignore* or *reject* God's existence, and thus end up being "without God."

What is wrong with Atheism?

At first sight, agnosticism—"we don't *know* if God exists"—seems to be the most harmless form of atheism. It merely *questions* God's existence. But its perceived mildness may prove to be a very deceiving misconception.

Although agnostics swear by the power of logic, but logic may not be the best tool to prove that God doesn't exist. G.K. Chesterton once said, "Atheism is the most daring of all dogmas, for it is the assertion of a universal negative." Chesterton is right; it is much easier to establish that there is a black swan somewhere on the earth than to prove that there isn't one at all (just keep searching). It might be true that God's existence cannot be proved in an empirical, scientific sense (as agnosticism asserts), but it is very hard, if not logically impossible, to conclude that God is in fact absent (as atheism claims). It is just impossible to close a search for God with the conclusion that there is no God. No searches ever conclusively reveal the absence of their object (just keep searching). Absence of evidence is not evidence of absence. On the other hand, the famous proofs of God's existence prove on compelling rational and metaphysical grounds that God must exist.

We discussed that issue earlier. But perhaps it is helpful here to paraphrase one of the proofs of God's existence in very general terms. How can we explain the existence of anything, including our own existence? We may go into biological causes, which we then can trace back to chemical causes, which in turn can be derived from physical causes. But all these causes combined don't really explain anything. For the entire chain of causes is just floating in the air, and it keeps doing so until we find a "foundation" for it to rest on or a "hook" for it to hang on. That's where the need for the First Cause comes in, which explains why all the other causes are only secondary causes in need of a First Cause, God.

So should we really remain undecided the way agnostics want us to? Catholic philosophers such as Peter Kreeft point out that agnosticism's demand for evidence pro or con God's existence degrades God, the Supreme Being, to our own level. They argue that the question of God should be treated differently from other knowable objects in that this question regards not that which is *below* us, but that which is *above* us. For one thing, God is a Primary Cause, not a secondary cause. The question "Does God exist?" is not like "Do neutrinos exist?" God cannot be "trapped" by some kind of ingenious experiment, for God is not a secondary cause. So how should we assess agnosticism then?

It may appear to be pretty harmless at first sight. But there is reason to question this impression. First of all, since agnosticism keeps us in limbo, it refuses to give God the honor and worship he deserves as our Maker. Agnostics never gave God their time to study the evidence that points to him. Of course, one can be an agnostic in other things than religion; many people are agnostics, for instance, when it comes to the existence of flying saucers or extraterrestrial life, because they never took the time to study such issues or to weigh the arguments pro and con. In other words, they are agnostics out of lack of interest. But when it comes to God, lack of interest is a much more serious case. We owe God our interest. But that assumes already that God exists, of course.

Here is a second reason why agnosticism may not be as harmless as it looks. While sitting on the fence—not sure if there is a God—agnostics often act as if they are very sure there is *no* God. They are theoretically agnostics, but practically atheists. But there is more. Very often agnostics do have a rather negative and highly selective attitude towards religion and religious people in particular—they tend to declare them "stupid." Agnostics think that their own logic is so compelling that everyone who disagrees with their agnostic conclusions must be misinformed or just brainless. So they often call religious people superstitious—believers in something unknown.

Accusing Christianity of superstition is often a cheap alibi agnostics use to reject it. It has been said many times that agnostics prefer to remain "sitting on the fence." But how long can one keep sitting there? At the end of life, a coin is being spun that will come down heads (God) or tails (no God). How will you wager? Peter Kreeft describes Pascal's Wager as follows: "If God does not exist, it does not matter how you wager, for there is nothing to win after death and nothing to lose after death. But if God does exist, your only chance of winning eternal happiness is to believe, and your only chance of losing it is to refuse to believe." In other words, agnosticism is a terrible bet, for it gives you no chance of winning. As Pascal said about belief in God, "If you gain, you gain all. If you lose, you lose nothing."

Why is agnosticism an impossible option? The reason is simple, in the words of Peter Kreeft again: "Because we are moving. The ship of life is moving along the waters of time, and there comes a point of no return, when our fuel runs out, when it is too late. The Wager works because of the fact of death." The option of not to wager at all is out of the question; each one of us has no choice but to wager in the face of death, given the possibility that we might be judged by God after death. So by "sitting on the fence," agnostics actually wager *against* God. It could be said that by refusing to choose, one has already chosen to wager on the idea that picking no religion is safer than accepting a false one.

But no matter how we define agnosticism, it should be criticized as a limitation of the mind's capacity to know reality. It actually limits the mind's capacity to know reality to the narrow viewpoint of logic, Relativism, Secularism, or Materialism. There *is* no God, agnostics say, because we cannot see him; there are no human souls because we cannot detect them physically; there is no God because we cannot empirically or scientifically prove the "God-hypothesis." Apparently, agnostics ignore the metaphysical proofs of

God's existence.

However, these agnostics do not realize that God's existence is not some kind of working hypothesis that we tentatively and provisionally hold on to until more evidence for or against it emerges. Instead, belief in God is of a different nature. It is more like saying about a spouse, parent, or friend, "I *know* he or she loves me"—which is certainly not a hypothesis either. Those who hold on to their faith do not resolve to let nothing count against their belief, but instead they have reason to keep their faith in spite of some seeming counter-evidence. Belief in God expresses someone's faith and commitment, which cannot possibly be tentative without undermining the very faith it means to express.

The second form of atheism—"we *cannot* know if God exists"—is much more serious and definite. It explicitly *denies* God's existence and declares it a delusion. These atheists want us to *believe* that believing in God is just impossible because science has shown us there *is* no God. They tend to believe that modern science is on their side. In their view, science and religion cannot go together. The philosopher Peter Kreeft reminds us of that Western in which one cowboy says to the other: "This town ain't big enough for both of us. One of us has to leave." Well, these atheists like to declare science as the winner, so religion has to leave town. They replace the trust religious believers place in God with the total trust they place in science—Scientism, that is (see Chapter 12). But we should question this view as we did earlier: How could science ever prove on its own that science is the only way of finding truth?

This kind of atheism denies everything that can't be dissected, counted, measured, or quantified, including God—and including itself, of course. Science on its own cannot answer questions that are beyond the reach of its empirical and experimental techniques. Nonetheless, these atheists keep promoting their dogma of Scientism, which includes the dogma that there are no dogmas, and ultimately no God. As a consequence, they acknowledge only one territory—the territory of science. Whatever it is that science gains must therefore be at the cost of religion.

In their view, scientific expansion means religious withdrawal—so religion must be on its way out whenever science advances. But that is exactly where the misconception lies. Science doesn't gain territory at all when it makes new discoveries, but it just learns more and more details about its own fixed and demarcated territory—which is the domain of all that can be dissected, counted, measured, and quantified. The rest is not part of its territory but was given away for other "authorities" to handle.

Therefore, scientists need to keep their scientific hands off of other domains, including the religious domain—which makes for a sound separation between Science and Religion. Science should never forget that it is "blind" for many other than scientific aspects of life. We mentioned earlier what Erwin Schrödinger once said about science, "It knows nothing of beautiful and ugly, good or bad, God and eternity. Science sometimes pretends to answer questions in these domains, but the answers are very often so silly that we are not inclined to take them seriously."

Because God is the Primary Cause, God could never be discovered among the secondary causes of this Universe, for God is not one of them. Science is about secondary causes, not the Primary Cause. God is outside its scope, just as everything else that is unseen and cannot be counted or measured is outside its scope. It is scientific arrogance to claim universal validity for local successes in science—in defiance of the fact that the astonishing successes of science have not been gained by answering every kind of question, but precisely by refusing to do so. God cannot be "seen" through telescopes or microscopes. Because God is everywhere, it only appears as if God is "nowhere." That is why there's no reason for megalomania in science. We always need to keep asking for "the rest of the story," for all those things science is "blind" for, including the existence of God.

The troubling part is that an atheist such as Richard Dawkins has never written a single word about God; what he talks about is some kind of demiurge—a being among other beings, who differs at best from all other beings in magnitude, power, and duration, but not a Primary Cause (see Chapter 2). If Dawkins decides not to believe in God, he should at least have a clear idea of what it is he claims not to believe in. This is a problem with many atheists—they often don't tell you what the god is they are rejecting. They may have a distorted picture of God in mind that is not the God Christianity believes in. So atheists owe us, and themselves, an explanation of what it is they reject—even if they do so in the name of science.

Apparently, science in itself is not the problem for religion. Reality tells us that there are atheistic scientists as well as religious scientists. Atheistic scientists are no better scientists than religious scientists, nor vice-versa. They both are dedicated scientists who believe in the power of the scientific method. But they differ in one thing. The latter keep an open mind and believe also in the power of religious faith, whereas the former close their mind for anything that cannot be dissected, counted, measured, or quantified. In either case, though, it is not science itself that can decide what the right choice is. Such a decision is a matter of "faith." Therefore, it is not science that "kills God," but rather particular scientists who do so in a very unscientific way.

Some people have an entirely different reason for saying

that we cannot know if God exists. Their reasoning is not based on science but on some kind of philosophy. If the Primary Cause is different from the secondary causes we are familiar with, so they reason, we cannot use the same terms for both of them. Consequently, the most we could say about God is that he is *not* what we know about secondary causes— *not* material, *not* .... So we can only speak about God in purely negative terms—"God is *not* this... and God is *not* that..." But if that were true, then we could not even say that God exists, for that is an affirmative rather than negative statement. A negative definition of God proceeds by elimination—it can begin, it can go on indefinitely, but it can never do its job. So there must be more to it.

What is the solution then for this problem? The terms we use for God are neither completely literal (or *univocal*, e.g. a dog is an "animal" and a cat is an "animal") nor are they completely different (or *equivocal*, e.g. a "bat" flying in the sky and a "bat" used in a game). Instead they are used in an intermediate sense (or *analogical*, e.g. a "good" story and a "good" person). In other words, God does "exist," but not the way creatures "exist." God also "causes" things to exist, but not in the same sense as a creature "causes" things. Terms like these are used in an analogical sense.

So the negative approach about God is indeed part of the story, but it cannot be the whole story—otherwise it would undermine the very arguments that led us to affirm that there is a God in the first place. That would make for a flawed conclusion. In other words, we can say much more about God in a positive way than these atheists want us to believe on logical or philosophical grounds. We cannot deny God by claiming that we do not know anything positive about God.

The third form of atheism—"we don't *care* to know if God exists"—seems rather subdued and remains eerily silent. It just *ignores* God's existence and never mentions God. Can we do so?

Of course, we can, for our Creator gave us that freedom. We are free to choose and embrace this kind of atheism, making us no longer sense any need to protest or even deny God's existence, because we are completely absorbed by what we can see, feel, hear, and touch in our surroundings. As far as God is concerned: out of "sight," out of mind. Since God is not someone to capture with our senses, God has become a "non-entity" in this world, making us blind for what cannot be seen and deaf for what cannot be heard.

We should really question the claim that there is no space for what we cannot see. Not only has science been masterful in discovering things we never thought existed, but science has also come up with entities that cannot be "seen" or "touched." We all experience gravity in life but we cannot see it (that is, until Newton came along); we know there is energy but it is invisible. There may be so much more to life than what "meets the eye." Not being able to see or touch some specific entities does not necessarily negate that they exist. The invisible or the unseen may very well be as real and factual as what is visible and seen. The invisible or the unseen seem even necessary for us to better see and understand the visible and seen things. To use a simple example: You can visit several buildings of Oxford University, but you can never visit Oxford University itself; it is not a building that can be "seen," yet it is a very real entity, vital to understanding the "unseen and invisible" unity behind all the "seen and visible" university buildings combined.

Once applied to religion, this opens up a wide and rich domain of "invisible things" that are so vital to Christianity. It is called the *spiritual* realm—the super-natural world behind the natural world, if you will. God is the Creator of "what is seen *and* unseen," of "what is visible *and* invisible," as the Nicene Creed puts it. We need to look beyond the natural to see the supernatural, beyond the present to see the eternal, beyond the visible to see the invisible, beyond the material to see the spiritual, beyond the secondary causes to see the Primary Cause. This does require faith, but certainly not "blind" faith. St. Paul made it clear that we can see the invisible God *through* the visible: "his invisible nature ... has been clearly perceived in the things that have been made" (Rom. 1:20).

Can God really be "out of sight" and "out of mind"? Perhaps he can, but for how long? What can we do when disaster strikes us, when things do not go the way we had planned, when we become victims of injustice in our man-made systems—in short, when self-made people reach their own limits? Don't we all know that life doesn't owe us a living? Suffering actually shows us that we are not in control of our lives but need divine assistance. In addition, we should ask these hidden atheists: isn't it striking that Christianity actually has the Cross at center stage in its religion; it claims there is some mysterious salvation for us in carrying our crosses in life—for the benefit of ourselves and the benefit of others. No wonder the Cross is a touchstone for Christians, but at the same time a stumbling block for non-Christians, including atheists.

Another reason why these atheists ignore God is that they suffer "religious amnesia." Let's keep in mind that, for centuries, it was unthinkable in the Western world to even deny God's existence. Although atheists are still a tiny, yet very vocal and growing minority in the Western World (approximately 4% in the USA), our society is changing fast. More and more people have no memory of the way life used to be; they live obliviously in complete religious ignorance. They are quietly leading a life of religious amnesia—aimless and clueless. It is a life of heathens. The bottom has been taken out of their lives—and they don't even know it. They are spiritually illiterate. They never give God or religion any thought. David Bentley Hart is right, "The reason the very concept of God has become at once so impoverished ... is not because of all the interesting things we have learned over the past few centuries, but because of all the vital things we have forgotten." When Aleksandr Solzhenitsyn, in his 1983 Templeton Prize lecture, tried to locate the root of the evils of the 20th century—two world wars, three totalitarian regimes with death camps, and a Cold War—he discerned a profound truth: "Men have forgotten God."

It is not that many of these heathens explicitly dismiss any basic kind of faith in God. They do not dismiss it, for one cannot dismiss what one has never received. They just never heard of it or never thought of it. It never crossed their minds. They have no way of seeing the world through the eyes of religious faith because they were never given that opportunity. When schools create graduates that are illiterate, we protest, but somehow we accept that schools, including the "school of family life," creates "graduates" who are spiritually illiterate. As the Communications expert Robert P. Lockwood puts it, "Children without faith not only become adults without faith, but adults who will pass that faithlessness on to their children." Tradition means literally: something we "pass or hand on." Unfortunately, our culture doesn't appreciate what has been handed on to us, because it is often considered second-hand.

And besides, since the existence of our world is contingent, not a necessity, our world would be nothing, literally, if there were no God. Without God, there is a permanent void in our lives—a void that may easily go unnoticed because it is a void. In the words of Pope Benedict XVI, "Again and again man falls behind the faith and wants to be just himself again; he becomes a heathen in the most profound sense of the word." These "heathens" of the atheistic type just don't care to believe in God because they think they are completely self-sufficient. They are not interested in God, because such a God would undermine the power of Man, the power of "Me, myself, and I."

The Catechism (2126) considers this "a false conception of human autonomy, exaggerated to the point of refusing any dependence on God." Autonomy does not mean that we can become whatever we please, without being accountable to anyone. Autonomy means instead that we become more and more aware of our deepest self. We understand ourselves best in the light of God. In one of her novels, Flannery O'Connor gave a good description of what this kind of atheism leads to: "Where you come from is gone, where you thought you were going to never was there, and where you are is no good unless you can get away from it. Where is there a place for you to be? No place." There is this gravestone of an atheist in the town of Thurmont, MD that could not express things better: "Here lies an Atheist. All dressed up and no place to go." That's where life without God ends.

The fourth form of atheism—"we don't *want* to know if God exists"—is probably the most belligerent form of atheism. It actively *rejects* God's existence.

What is going on here? The philosopher William Lane Craig gives us a plausible answer: "No one in the final analysis fails to become a Christian because of a lack of arguments; he fails to become a Christian because he loves darkness rather than light and wants nothing to do with God." The key line here is that such a person "wants nothing to do with God"; he wants no part of the Light, but cherishes the darkness instead. It is the will, says Blaise Pascal, which "dissuades the mind from considering those aspects it doesn't like to see." One could say in general that if someone vehemently rejects God, it is almost impossible for such person to be won over by any kind of empirical evidence or rational arguments.

Take the atheist biologist Richard Lewontin and self-proclaimed Marxist who once defended materialism when he wrote, "[W]e cannot allow a Divine Foot in the door." The keyword is "allow": If we would *allow* that, then... Apparently, we are dealing here with a choice made before evidence is brought in. Atheists often invest a great deal of time and energy in fleeing the very God they reject. But isn't flight itself the recognition that there is something from which to flee? There is actually aversion, disgust, and even hatred involved. So the pivotal question is this: what is behind the deep-seated hatred that these atheists nurse against religion and against God?

Let's face it, there is only one force that hates God's Creation more than anything else—and that force is Satan. Satan is not an atheist in the regular sense. Satan knows that God exists but wants no part of him. He rejects God and refuses to acknowledge him. It is Satan's ultimate goal to demolish all Christian elements in society and to damage the human image that was made in God's image. Satan prowls about the world for the ruin of souls. He is not literally an atheist himself, yet his hatred of God loves to spread atheism.

Could Satan be the real instigator of this aggressive form of atheism? It is hard to say "no" to this question. As a matter of fact, destructive atheism could very well be part of a much larger picture—a cosmic warfare, so to speak, between Good and Evil, between God and Satan. It is God's aim for each one of us to attain Heaven after death, whereas Satan's aim is to ensure that as many people as possible miss that eternal goal. Do not take God and Satan as two eternal principles locked in permanent conflict as in Gnosticism (see Chapter

3), for Satan and other demons are fallen Angels who were originally created good by God, but they decided in their freedom to go against their Creator. Obviously, Satan is a reality; and evil is something real to watch out for. God can do so much good when we let him. And Satan can do so much evil when we let him.

It is only the religious "eye" that sees all of history as a cosmic and constant warfare between God and Satan, waged everywhere and daily—"24/7." It "sees" how life is more of a battleground than a playground. It "sees" how the power of evil and the light of Satan enabled men such as Hitler, Stalin, Mao, bin Laden, and ISIS to spellbind and enslave the minds and spirits of millions, creating hell ahead of time, right here on earth. This explains how such people could have sold their souls by following "orders" that stem from sources far beyond their own resources. Only religious people are able to see this dimension in history that historians usually miss. They are able to see what is unseen behind all that is seen.

And now we witness again how the power of evil, the "light" of Satan, is enabling *atheists* to spellbind and enslave the minds and spirits of millions, creating havoc on earth with religious erosion and mudslides. These atheists have been happy to sell their souls to their new "master." No wonder the reality of evil goes far beyond material and physical powers; it goes even far beyond what human beings can do on their own. Aleksandr Solzhenitsyn is very adamant about the way atheistic communism operated in the former Soviet Union: "Militant atheism is not merely incidental or marginal to Communist policy; it is not a side effect, but the central pivot." Whether it is Stalin or Mao or Hitler or bin Laden or ISIS, the key question is: could they have ever done what they did relying on their own human power alone? The answer seems to be a definite "no."

This explains how such people can follow "orders"

stemming from sources far beyond their own resources. They churn out endless propaganda against God through books, mass media, and the internet—and are rather successful in doing so. The fuel behind all their convictions is some satanic force engaged in a battle against God's creation—which is the role of Satan, the "father" of all lies, the great divider who knows how to remain hidden behind the scene. Satan is happy to lend such people some "spiritual" help from "beyond." That is why these atheists seem to feel empowered from "on high" to declare to the whole world that there is no God, and that they are "his prophets." But we should really question whose prophets they are.

Some side effects of Atheism

Now that we know what is wrong with the various forms of atheism, we may see better why atheism has not been able to get rid of God and God's existence. We should always maintain that God either exists or he does not exist. Our belief in him cannot make God appear, nor can our disbelief in him make God disappear. Atheism can only cause an "eclipse" of God. Think of a solar eclipse, for instance. The eclipse does not make the sun literally vanish; instead it makes the sun temporarily invisible for us. The same is true of atheism. It does not make God literally vanish; instead it makes God temporarily invisible for us. Atheism may be able to change people's minds but it cannot change the reality of the world we live in. We are like the moon: we produce no light on our own but merely reflect the light of God.

What makes us so sure that this God really exists? Without God, there would be no basis for our world and for our individual lives to even exist. Nothing could exist if there were no God. We cannot avoid asking ourselves, "Why is there something rather than nothing?" The question was once worded this way by the German philosopher Gottfried Leibniz. He used to say that the sufficient reason, which needs no further reason, must be outside of this series of contingent things and is found in a necessary Being bearing the reason for its existence within itself. Only God can be this Being. Only God can bring us, and the world, into being and keep us, and the world, into being. When God creates, he does not change a no-thing into a some-thing, nor does he change something into something else—like chemists change water into hydrogen and oxygen. Instead, when God creates, he brings everything into being and existence.

But there is so much more to ensure to us that God exists. How else are we to explain the fact that there is order, design, fine-tuning, intelligibility, rationality, and morality in this Universe? How could nature be intelligible if it were not created by an intelligent Creator? How could there be order in this world if there were no "orderly" Creator? How could there be scientific laws in nature if there were no rational Lawgiver? How could there be design in nature, if there were no intelligent Designer? How could there be human minds, if there is no Mind behind the Universe?

We have a choice here when answering these rhetorical questions: we either accept that there is no explanation at all for these observations in nature—which is basically irrational and absurd—or we look for a rational explanation for all of this. I would argue that the best, if not the only, rational explanation seems to be that there is indeed an intelligent, rational, orderly, and lawgiving Creator God who made this Universe the way it is—and thus made it fit for us to live in. If someone still objects that things may just have no explanation, then we should respond, "I just gave you an explanation."

If there is no creative Mind behind the Universe, how would we explain the human mind? Without God, we would

almost literally lose our mind. All that we believe to be true
and all that we believe to be right can only be trusted if there
is a God, the Maker of truths and untruths, rights and
wrongs. Individually, these elements may not provide
conclusive evidence, but combined they make for a strong
case in favor of God. This may not be a matter of provability
but at least of credibility. Belief in God makes the world so
much more understandable. C. S. Lewis beautifully summarized this, "I believe in Christianity as I believe that the
sun has risen: not only because I see it, but because by it I
see everything else." Indeed, belief in God puts everything in
a clear light.

Let's face it: If there were no intelligent Creator, how
could nature be intelligible for us? If there were no "orderly"
Creator, where would the order of this world come from? If
there were no rational Lawgiver, how could there be
scientific laws in nature? If there were no intelligent
Designer, where could the design of nature come from? If
there were no Mind behind the Universe, how could there be
human minds? Without God's Mind, there would only be
mere chaos, or actually nothing.

More in general, we have reason now to say there would
be no basis for our rationality and no basis for our morality,
if there were no God. Without God, there would not be
anything true or false in rationality, nor anything right or
wrong in morality. There would be no absolute standards,
neither for truths and untruths nor for rights and wrongs. All
that we believe to be true and all that we believe to be right
can only be trusted if there is a God, the Maker of truths and
untruths, rights and wrongs. Without God, everything would
be completely equivalent in being worth nothing.

It should be clear by now which disastrous effects
atheism has had for our world and for us. Given all of the
above, we must come to the conclusion that atheism—in

questioning, denying, ignoring, or rejecting God's existence—has opened the door widely to all the destructive doctrines we discussed in this book.

16.   Conclusion

There have always been false and destructive doctrines. Some are old, some have disappeared, some are new. We as Christians or Catholics live in a world with its own false and destructive doctrines. That's why it is often said that we may not be "*of* the world," but are still "*in* the world."

That has always been so. Here is a priceless gem, the *Epistle to Diognetus*, which we are most fortunate to have as only one copy survived the centuries. We do not know who wrote it. It came from the second century, from one of the earliest Christians. It was, like the New Testament, originally written in Greek. In this brief excerpt we have preserved a magnificent description of Christian living, of what life was like in the early church community which had to deal with various false and destructive doctrines surrounding them during that time. It also tells us what life is like for modern Christians of this age:

They dwell in their own countries, but simply as sojourners. As citizens, they share in all things with others and yet endure all things as if foreigners. Every foreign land is to them as their native country, and every land of their birth as a land of strangers. They marry, as do all others; they beget children; but they do not destroy their offspring. They have a common table, but not a common bed. They are in the flesh, but they do not live after the flesh. They pass their days on earth, but they are citizens of heaven. They obey the prescribed laws, and at the same time surpass the laws by their lives. They love all men and are persecuted by all. They are unknown and condemned; they are put to death and restored to life. They are poor yet make many rich; they are in lack of all things and yet abound in all; they are dishonored and yet in their very dishonor are glorified. They are evil spoken of and yet are justified; they are reviled and bless; they are insulted and repay the insult with honor; they do good yet are punished as evildoers. ... To sum it all up in one word—what the soul is to the body, that are Christians in the world.

Endorsements

"A compelling critique of false ideas that disturb our minds even when we don't even know they are infiltrating us! In 50 years of teaching why the errors refuted in this book are false, I have never come upon a more concise explanation than Verschuuren's."

— Ronda Chervin, Professor Emerita, Holy Apostles College & Seminary, Cromwell, CT

"Phenomenal engagement of the most relevant issues of our day! A must-read for our students and graduates!"

— Dr. Sebastian Mahfood, OP, Trustee of Aquinas Institute of Theology, St Louis, MO

Index

About the Author

 Gerard M. Verschuuren is a human biologist, specialized in human genetics. He also earned a doctorate in the philosophy of science. He studied and worked at universities in Europe and the United States. Currently semi-retired, he spends most of his time as a writer, speaker, and consultant on the interface of science and religion, faith and reason.

Some of his most recent books are:

* *God and Evolution?—Science Meets Faith.* (Boston, MA: Pauline Books, 2012).
* *The Destiny of the Universe—In Pursuit of the Great Unknown.* (St. Paul, MN: Paragon House, 2014).
* *Five Anti-Catholic Myths—Slavery, Crusades, Inquisition, Galileo, Holocaust.* (Kettering, OH: Angelico Press, 2015).
* *Life's Journey—A Guide from Conception to Growing Up, Growing Old, and Natural Death.* (Kettering, OH: Angelico Press, 2016).
* *Aquinas and Modern Science—A New Synthesis of Faith and Reason.* (Kettering, OH: Angelico Press, 2016).
* *Faith and Reason—The Cradle of Truth.* (St. Louis, MO: En Route Books and Media, 2017).

- *The Myth of an Anti-Science Church—Galileo, Darwin, Teilhard, Hawking, Dawkins.* (Kettering, OH: Angelico Press, 2018).
- *The First Christians—Keeping the Faith in Times of Trouble.* (St. Louis, MO: En Route Books and Media, 2018).
- *The Eclipse of God—Is Religion on the Way out?* (St. Louis, MO: En Route Books and Media, 2018).
- *Forty Anti-Catholic Lies.* (Manchester, NH: Sophia Institute Press, 2018.
- *Broken Hearts in a Broken World.* (St. Louis, MO: En Route Books and Media, 2018).
- *In the Beginning*-How God Made Earth Our Home. (Manchester, NH: Sophia Institute Press, 2019).

For more info:
http://en.wikipedia.org/wiki/Gerard_Verschuuren.

He can be contacted at www.where-do-we-come-from.com.